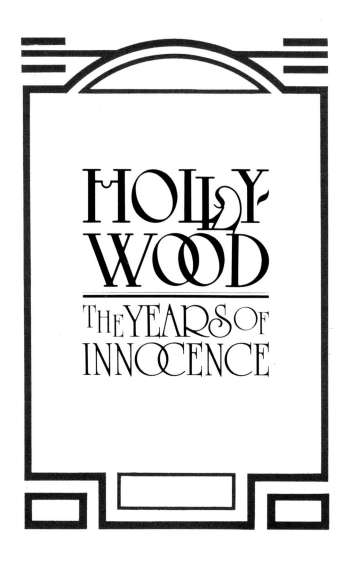

HOLLY WOOD

THE YEARS OF INNOCENCE

Mary Pickford, "America's Sweetheart," in 1916.

HOLLY WOOD
THE YEARS OF INNOCENCE

JOHN KOBAL

INTRODUCTION BY KEVIN BROWNLOW

Thames and Hudson

©1985 Thames and Hudson Ltd, London

Illustrations © 1985 The Kobal Collection

Printed and bound in Hungary

Contents

Introduction

The idea of Hollywood as a boomtown would not have surprised those who lived there as this century began, for they worked hard toward that very ideal. But they would have been astounded and dismayed had they foreseen the kind of boomtown it was destined to become.

In 1886 Mr and Mrs Harvey Henderson Wilcox acquired a fig orchard in a remote suburb of Los Angeles called Cahuenga Valley. Los Angeles, an expanding city of fifty thousand inhabitants, was enjoying a real estate boom, thanks to the Southern Pacific Railroad connection, which linked the city directly with the East. Wilcox found himself paying one hundred and fifty dollars an acre for land that had cost less than two dollars an acre a few years earlier. Mrs Wilcox, engaging in pleasantries with a fellow passenger on a train journey east, was charmed by the name of the lady's summer home, Hollywood. Mrs Wilcox adopted the English-sounding name, and upon her return, the Cahuenga Valley-Wilcox Ranch became Hollywood Ranch. Mr Wilcox, with the literal mind of a Kansas Prohibitionist, sought to justify

Looking south from the Hollywood Hills, c. 1896. "Lemon and orange orchards . . . stretched across the valley, interspersed with market gardens."

the name by importing some English holly. The holly seemed to be the only plant in the entire valley that refused to flourish; it withered and died.

Horticulture was a sideline for Mr Wilcox, whose passion and profession was real estate. He amused himself by subdividing his property, laying out streets in strict rectangles and lining them with pepper trees. He decorated his office in Los Angeles with an impressive map of Hollywood. The original settlers in Cahuenga Valley were not consulted about the change of name. Wilcox was also able to select his neighbors. A wealthy Colorado miner, inspired by a few flourishing lemon trees on the Wilcox ranch, bought some lots and laid out a lemon orchard, adding to it an imposing mansion. But when a Frenchman named Blondeau bought six acres at Sunset Boulevard and Gower Street, intending to open a saloon, Wilcox threatened to cancel the deal. Nevertheless, Blondeau in time managed to establish a roadhouse serving meals and liquor. This delighted some of the other residents, for their aim was to spread the name of Hollywood throughout the land, and to achieve this aim many tourists were necessary. Lemon and orange orchards soon stretched across the valley, interspersed with market gardens. Twelve thousand trees were planted in 1896 alone; samples of the fruit placed on

display in Los Angeles were so impressive that the eagerly awaited tourists began arriving.

The Cahuenga Valley inspired those wealthy enough to maintain two homes to establish winter residences there. Asthmatic Easterners moved to this Eden for their health. One prospective purchaser was shocked by the high cost of Hollywood real estate; four hundred dollars an acre seemed excessive. Thirty days later, when he asked for "the best buy in Hollywood," the price had soared to six hundred dollars. He pointed out that since he had rejected the land at four hundred dollars an acre, he was hardly likely to accept it at six hundred dollars. Thirty days later he learned the price was eight hundred dollars. "My," he said, "That's a bitter pill to swallow, but I believe I'll take it." He bought.

A local improvement society demanded "charity . . . more enthusiasm, more kindly feeling for all. More flowers and greater beauty, broad avenues shaded with ornamental trees." They demanded, too, a lively press agent to keep the advantages of the area before the public. One of those advantages came from the valley's richest man, Colonel Griffith J. Griffith, a Welshman who had made his fortune as a mining engineer and owned the huge Rancho Los Feliz. In 1896 he had donated over three thousand acres to the city of Los Angeles to be used as a park – then the largest city park in the world.

The fame of the little community for its park and for its orchards was eclipsed by the arrival of Paul De Longpré, the French painter of flowers. Mr Wilcox's widow offered to sell him an estate on Cahuenga Avenue – with the provision that he establish a studio there. He agreed, but finding the place too small, he bought a lot on Hollywood Boulevard, for which he paid the delighted Mrs Wilcox with three paintings. He built a Moorish mansion, crowned with cupolas, and surrounded it with a garden of such beauty that it became one of the prime showplaces of Southern California. The handful of tourists who visited the orchards multiplied to thousands yearly coming to see the artist and his dazzling garden. Newspapers praised De Longpré and his work, bringing Hollywood immense prestige. Many tourists fell in love with the place, purchased lots, and built homes, and in gratitude to the Frenchman who attracted them, the city named a street in his honor – De Longpré Avenue.

Most of the other streets were named after the original subdividers – Gower Street, Curson Avenue, McCadden Place. When H.J. Whitley opened his "Hollywood Ocean View" tract with immense ceremony, stockholders and prospective buyers admired the fine homes in the course of construction and toured the new Hollywood Hotel. The emotion of the day was expressed by one of the organizers, who declared with a sweeping gesture, "Behold what God hath wrought." A little later a group of real estate agents offered Whitley a stretch of rough land in lieu of money they

A typical turn-of-the-century mansion in one of Hollywood's "better" neighborhoods.

owed him: as Whitley Heights it became some of the most sought after acreage in town.

Hollywood's rapid growth was reflected in the little Pass School, whose three rooms were soon impossibly overcrowded, not so much from the local birthrate as from immigration. To accommodate the new population, Hollywood High School was constructed in 1904.

The city fathers took care to ensure that the expansion was in line with their intentions. They banned the sale of liquor, except by pharmacists, and passed ordinances to prohibit slaughterhouses, glue factories, and gasworks within the city limits. When it was proposed that the streetcar fare from Los Angeles be cut, one of the city fathers declared that while the town needed more people, did it need the kind of person a five-cent fare would bring?

By carefully trying to preserve the dignified character of the town, the city fathers ensured its destruction. Thanks to their prohibition on liquor, the Blondeau roadhouse suffered a crippling loss of revenue, and Mrs Blondeau was eager to lease it. The roadhouse had a barn, a corral, twelve cabins, and a bungalow. In October 1911 some motion-picture people from New Jersey were directed there by a local photographer, and the Blondeaus leased the place for thirty dollars a month. The newcomers put horses in the corral, props in the barn, turned the cabins into dressing rooms and the

The first motion-picture studio in Hollywood, formerly the Blondeau roadhouse, at Sunset and Gower.

bungalow into offices, and established the first motion-picture studio in Hollywood.

They called themselves the Nestor Film Company. The owners, two brothers from England – David and William Horsley – had also called themselves the Centaur Film Company when they worked in Bayonne, New Jersey. They had been refused a license by the Motion Picture Patents Company, a trust headed by the Edison company, which attempted to wipe out competition by claiming a monopoly on patents. In common with other outfits, Centaur was harassed by Patents Company agents who used violence when the law failed to work fast enough. Now Centaur wanted to get as far as possible from the East Coast. The California weather was a strong inducement, but they were also attracted by the wild country close to Hollywood, into which they could disappear at the mere sniff of a Patents agent. As a last resort, the Mexican border was not too far away.

Nestor began shooting very quickly, and the fine weather enabled them to keep to a rapid schedule. They had no facilities for making prints, so they shipped their negatives to New York. When the results were seen and word got about, more and more so-called independents made the decision to go to California, and many arrived in Hollywood. These were the very men the city fathers strove to avoid – the ex-secondhand clothes dealers, poolroom proprietors, blacksmiths, fish merchants. And in their wake came an even more regrettable class of people – actors.

Retired people, who had moved to Hollywood to enjoy its tranquility, were deeply upset when curious wooden stages appeared on unrestricted property adjoining their homes, to the sound of furious and apparently endless hammering. The owners of these things never seemed satisfied; no sooner had they erected one interior than they tore it down and built another. A closer look revealed people, painted like street-walkers, contorting themselves in agonized gestures before painted canvas. The staccato click of the cameras, the bellowing of the directors, and the hammering of the carpenters depressed the local citizens, whose ideal of art was the gentle brushstroke of Paul De Longpré.

The city hastily passed a zoning ordinance to prevent further structures from defacing the landscape. Thus Hollywood escaped the fate of becoming the center of moving-picture production. The early temporary stages gave way to more sophisticated studios, which were built in outlying areas like Edendale, Boyle Heights, and Culver City. But the attractive name of Hollywood sprang to mind long before the names of such obscure places, and it soon became the generic term for the film-producing area of Southern California. Neighboring towns eventually submitted to its fame themselves; Toluca and Lankershim became North Hollywood, while Ivanhoe and Prospect Park became East Hollywood. There were West and South Hollywood as well.

Yet in these early days the nerve center of the moving-picture industry was in downtown Los Angeles, at the Alexandria Hotel, where casting was carried on in the bar and deals were made in the lobby, on the carpet called "the million-dollar rug." The wealthier actors stayed here, or at the Rex Arms Apartments, or at the Hollywood Hotel. The stars, before World War I, lived modestly. The majestic homes still belonged to the oil millionaires, the mining tycoons, and the politicians. The more ordinary actors lived in cottages, bungalows, or apartments. Such was the prejudice against "movies" that at least one boarding-house advertised, "No dogs or actors." Many players soon to build themselves castles were satisfied with two rooms and a shared bathroom. Accustomed to stage life, they had been sustained by hotel rooms throughout their careers. "I never had a home in my life," said DeWolf Hopper, "until I came west."

Hollywood at this transitory period was, by all accounts, a delightful and exhilarating place. It was a pleasure to get up in the morning – which was just as well, because picture people were often required on location at six to catch the best of the light. The preponderance of retired people gave the place a drowsy and restful atmosphere. "The citizens," said Agnes de Mille, "spent long parts of the afternoons moving the sprinkler from one section of the lawn to another." A weekend drive would take in Beverly Hills, where sidewalks disappeared into open fields, lampposts indicated uninhabited streets, and nurseries glowed with poinsettias. The foothills, hazy purple turning brown in summer, darkened by heat waves and brush fires,

Cast and crew of *The Squaw Man* (1914), the film that launched ex-actor Cecil B. De Mille (extreme left) on his long career as a director. Above him sits his co-director, Oscar Apfel. The film's star, Dustin Farnum (hatless), and his leading lady, Princess Red Wing (at his left shoulder), are in the center of the truck, surrounded by some of the Indians who found work as extras and stuntmen in many of the early Westerns.

miraculously acquired a coat of green in the winter, a winter that was far too warm to deserve the name. "When people mention Hollywood," recalled Agnes de Mille, "I am not minded of the goings-on in the hot studios, nor the pleasant social life of cheap oranges and easy swims, but of the untouched country behind the town, pagan, pantheistic, where mountain cats still prowl, the little deer start and tremble at human approach, coyotes scream and the beneficent rain comes down in the eucalyptus groves."

The rain, rare as it was, proved a great inconvenience, and few of the temporary motion-picture structures could withstand it. The barn where the legendary Cecil B. De Mille, Agnes de Mille's uncle, made *The Squaw Man* in 1913 leaked, so when it rained, De Mille and Mamie Wagner, his film editor, took turns protecting each other with an umbrella. A downpour often brought the fledgling industry to a halt. Flash floods destroyed Universal's prestigious studio ranch soon after it opened – although, with typical Universal panache, they turned the disaster to advantage by filming a melodrama entitled *The Fate of the Flood Waters*.

The rains played such havoc with the roads that horses were favored above automobiles. Comparatively few people owned limousines, and a parked Rolls-Royce gathered a crowd. Lillian and Dorothy Gish, on the other hand, complained of people staring at them when they traveled to and from the Fine Arts studio on the streetcar. As the roads improved, the number of cars increased. Licenses were obtainable without a test, and any adult could drive. (There were a remarkable number of crashes for so small an automotive population.) But overcrowded roads were unknown, and

cars could travel unimpeded for blocks, side by side, the drivers chatting to one another.

However attractive the town and its climate, there were plenty of complaints, particularly from those accustomed to the conveniences of New York. The sewerage was bad, and when Los Angeles began supplying the tap water, it proved to be so alkaline that fresh water had to be delivered to the door in tanks. The beautiful pepper trees showered berries onto automobile hoods, and the juice damaged them; the pepper trees paid for this crime with their lives. Telephone operators listened in on the phone calls of the stars and created a spider's web of gossip. The old guard of original settlers were ambivalent in their attitude to those they referred to as "movies:" the vast sums of money spent brought unparalleled prosperity, but the intrusion of New York was resented. The sight of kosher restaurants and synagogues added fuel to their bigotry. Their desire to hold on to their past led to such anomalies as the exclusive Garden Court Apartments, which refused moving-picture people but could not resist the Old World conservatism of producer-director J. Stuart Blackton, or the enchanting innocence of Bessie Love.

In contrast to the settlers' curious mixture of kindness and snobbery, the moving-picture people adopted a casual democracy. "There is no class distinction in Hollywood," wrote Mary Winship in *Photoplay*. "The most rabid socialist can point to it as an example of communism as far as social usages are concerned. People who have money make a great to-do about it, of course. But it makes absolutely no difference to the relations of people.

De Mille in partnership with Jesse L. Lasky and Samuel Goldfish (later Goldwyn) had formed the Jesse L. Lasky Feature Play Company. *The Squaw Man*, their first production, was made in this studio at Selma and Vine, just off Hollywood Boulevard. In 1916 the company merged with Adolph Zukor's Famous Players Film Company to become Famous Players-Lasky Corporation. Later the name was changed to Paramount Pictures. The original barn, now designated a historical monument, has been moved to a location opposite the Hollywood Bowl, where it serves as a museum of early film-making in Los Angeles.

13

You are just as apt to meet every different occupation, position, and salary of man and woman at any party you go to. Some of the greatest friendships I have ever known in pictures exist between people of such radically different positions that it could not occur in other professions."

The freedom of women was another striking feature of pre-1920s Hollywood. Observers were both shocked and encouraged: "Not even Greenwich Village has achieved so great a freedom in this respect." Women could work, relax, and conduct their lives on the same basis as men. They could be found grinding cameras both for feature and newsreel companies, marshaling actors as directors, and organizing studios as producers. They were not present in any great numbers, but they made their mark, and the importance to early Hollywood of women in the executive class is notable. Mary Pickford may have been America's Sweetheart; she was also the highest salaried player-producer in the world.

To call the Hollywood life relaxing became increasingly inaccurate. The routine was easy enough in the days before studios employed artificial light; work finished at 4.30 as the light went yellow. But motion-pictures underwent enormous advances from 1911 to 1917, and with the advances went immense creative effort. Work may have stopped by mid-afternoon in the early days; a few years later it often dragged on past midnight. Streetcars stopped at ten, and Hollywood streets were dark and deserted, so

The old Hollywood Hotel on a still uncluttered Hollywood Boulevard, with the Hollywood Hills in the background. Newly arrived film folk would often stay here while they looked for homes to lease in the vicinity.

if you had no car and no horse, you walked home. Directors and actors congregated at the Green Room, if there was anything left of the evening. The wild life so beloved of Hollywood fiction belonged to weekends, although the great night at the Hollywood Hotel was Thursday. If you lived in Hollywood, you were welcome, and you could dance alongside Chaplin, the Gish sisters, Anita Loos, Constance and Norma Talmadge. The event was initiated by the light-opera star Richard Carle, who staged an impromptu evening so successfully that the hotel made a regular date of it. The lingering Prohibition, reimposed during the war, caused revelers to drive to outlying roadhouses, such as the self-styled Vernon Country Club. "They had the biggest bar in the world out there," recalled the stunt man Harvey Parry. "One time, Tom Mix came up with an old car he had, and drove it right through the door. He got to his feet in this loud cowboy outfit he wore and said, 'Tom Mix is my name. The drinks are on me.'"

The swashbuckling style aroused antipathy. Citizens were hotly indignant when prevented from crossing their own streets by aggressive assistants. They could not be expected to understand the danger – the road had been covered with soap and grease, and Keystone paddy wagons were about to screech past, skidding in endless circles. Dignified matrons were not flattered to be propositioned with five dollars to do a walk-on because they were the "perfect type." Most of them disapproved intensely of motion-pictures and went so far as to refuse permission for their houses to be photographed. Not that they were immune even then. A trained mule wandered away from a movie company on location and frightened an elderly resident with a playful nip. When she ran into her house, the mule followed – charging straight through the screen door. Movie "burglars" broke into the wrong house, terrifying the occupants. A bank was held up in true movie style, but the camera was phony and the actors real bandits. Cowboys galloped their horses over newly mown lawns, tearing up the grass. Citizens further complained that picture people bullied them in Griffith Park. But here again, the moviemakers' need for dangerous charges by cowboy cavalry could not be sacrificed for the sake of ramblers who had two thousand other acres to ramble in. Some of these residents exercised considerable power, however, and in 1915 picture companies were banned from private parks. Reacting with justifiable anger, and pointing to the five million dollars spent by the industry every year in the Los Angeles area, several companies hinted they might move to somewhere offering more encouragement and courtesy. At once the Merchants and Manufacturers Association linked arms to prevent this alarming loss of business. They acknowledged the tremendous advertising service provided by the movies, displaying the city's scenic beauties and climatic advantages to audiences all over the world, and passed a resolution deploring the obstacles placed by officials in the way of an industry so advantageous to Los Angeles.

This was all very well, declared the picture people, but it wasn't only the officials. The very merchants discriminated against them! The movies were making them rich, yet they retained their snobbery. A hasty meeting of the Chamber of Commerce and the producers was described as "a love feast" by the press, but the affection was both strained and temporary. The resentment continued. Well into the 1920s real estate agents assured their clients: "No movie people live on *this* street. There won't be any wild parties; you'll be assured of quiet." When they opened Bel-Air, a residential community, movie people were excluded. A country club went so far as to refuse to allow members to wear knickerbockers; they made them look too much like film directors.

And yet the movies brought the benefit the Chamber of Commerce had always striven for: tourism. To cope with the influx, the Chamber prepared a booklet that assured tourists that motion-picture studios were only a part of Hollywood – "lower Hollywood" – and were "more or less lost in the far-spreading bungalowed landscape." The only other evidence of movie business might be the presence on the sidewalk of a group of people, "a man turning the crank of a camera . . . while another man makes a girl do something foolish over and over again. Scenes like this attract little attention. The real Hollywood is engaged in its own affairs which are those

of ordinary everyday humanity, working and trading and living, and well satisfied to live in a beautiful place.''

The fan magazines attacked this attitude, calling its authors "Hollywood's Shameber of Commerce,'' but actually most studios were anxious to avoid visitors. Although Universal welcomed tourists at its vast studio ranch in the San Fernando Valley, the other studios were considerably less hospitable. Lacking the space of Universal, they had also suffered from a plague of souvenir hunters on the occasions they had admitted visitors. Objects vital to continuity vanished, and pictures were held up while identical articles were tracked down in town. Anything portable was automatically pillaged by eager star worshipers, and it proved safer to close the studio gates. The wonderful sets tourists had seen in pictures were denied them, and the exteriors of most studios were uniformly dull. In later years visitors were offered special tours of the stars' homes. But in the early days these were all too ordinary. "The trouble with Hollywood,'' said one disgruntled visitor, "is that it's so damn unimpressive.''

Some of the movie people felt the same way, despite the astonishing climate and the breathtaking scenery. When shots of New York appeared on the screen, you could identify members of the movie colony by their applause. "The heat gets on your nerves,'' said one, "It's so dusty you have to change your clothes three times a day and you're never clean.''

How quickly they came to change their minds! After the real estate explosions of the 1920s and 1930s, the quietness and simplicity of the early years were greatly missed.

The first studio to admit sightseers was Carl Laemmle's Universal, which brought busloads of tourists from Los Angeles to Universal City in the North Hollywood foothills to see how motion pictures were made. In this photo they are standing on an observation platform in the rear as they watch Fred Kelsey direct a scene from *Love's Lariat* (1916), starring Harry Carey. By 1917 the studio had discontinued its open-house policy, having decided that it was too much of a nuisance. But in the late 1950s, when movies were in a serious slump, Universal revived this practice, charging admission and reaping a small fortune.

Looking at the pictures in this book, the everyday quality is very striking. There is nothing spectacular about the community pictured here, however remarkable its work proved to be. But its lack of pretension seems immensely attractive, particularly in the light of what was to happen in Hollywood. Of this period Katherine Albert wrote: "Hollywood was a child, charming and naive. Now [in the 1930s] it is a woman of the world, sparkling, bizarre, hard and bitter, with a painted face and narrow eyes." For film enthusiasts, the Thirties have a charm of their own, which makes the description a period piece in itself – proving the dangers of uncritical nostalgia. But one can see what she meant. The pictures here of the gentle, sleepy days before the 1920s, before Hollywood reached its zenith as a hotbed of whoopee, capture not merely the charm and naiveté. They help to document a totally forgotten period. They serve as a vivid family album of the talented and energetic people to whom we, the film industry, pay tribute. And some of them, quite fortuitously, provide remarkable evidence of the photographer's art.

KEVIN BROWNLOW

Scottish-born Spottiswoode Aitken, one of D.W. Griffith's leading character actors (he played Dr Cameron in *Birth of a Nation*), taking his family on an outing in his shiny new Overland. The view from Sunset Boulevard sparkles in the smogless sunshine. Aitken was among the first of a long and distinguished line of British expatriates who found Hollywood's climate a distinct change for the better.

Nelson Evans, Photographer

Nelson Evans's studio
on Hollywood
Boulevard. The two-
storey structure
pictured here has long
since disappeared.

Every town has its photographers. By the time the nineteenth century gave way to the twentieth, almost every family, no matter how humble, had a picture of itself. Weddings, birthdays, confirmations – all the immortal days in mortal lives were captured in photographs. The precious faces of loved ones were caught and framed and given to be kept on mantelpieces.

Hollywood was no different, except that in the biggest small town in America every day was an event, each new film a happening. Stars and starlets needed photographs to keep their faces before the roving eyes of their fickle swains, the public, whose affection was as rapacious as it could prove inconstant. So Hollywood became a photographer's paradise. Soon after the film companies were established, they swarmed in to photograph the faces in search of fame. Only the best lasted – men like Witzel, Edwin Bower Hesser, Melbourne Spurr, Freulich, Henry Waxman, Ira Hill.

With them came Nelson H. Evans – not the first, but one of the best. He flourished in the 1910s and early 20s, and his pictures are the core and *raison d'être* of this book.

What charms in these early images – the bulk of them taken between 1915 and 1921 – is their freshness, a spontaneity that Hollywood never showed again. Their innocence is as much in Evans as in his subjects. The time captured is one of growth, of change: movies, people, cars – all caught in mid-step before they freeze into position. What grew into adulthood in the 1920s is pictured here at the awkward age of puberty. The stars that supplanted these were more regal, crystallized, remote, fantastic. Here, whether Bathing Beauty, Griffith Girl or would-be Mary Pickfords or Theda Baras, are countenances still open to suggestion, eyes still wide with astonishment. These are faces that parents and sweethearts could recognize, faces in which movie-struck hopefuls across the country saw themselves, prompting them to catch the next train to try their luck in dreamland.

The laughter in these faces radiates from the person, and is not conjured up to match an image or portray a mood. This exuberance is found not only in the famous or the remembered, but in those whose careers never survived the decade of the 1910s. There is hope in all of them. Whether they burned out quickly, or forever shone beneath the appellation of "Sennett Bathing Beauty" or "Griffith Girl," or later ascended to become luminaries in the 1920s doesn't matter. For them, for this time, anything could happen.

It was possible to take a tram to the Griffith studios and, with enough gumption and naivety, see the great man himself by pretending you had an appointment. Minutes later, you could find yourself at work in the movies.

Because it was possible, they came in hope from every town of the United States, although fan magazines from their earliest numbers carried articles discouraging hopefuls and their letter columns bulged with sad stories and awful warnings. But still they came to "make good" in the movies. It was the last frontier for the pioneer spirit. It was the first day, and your chances were as good as the next person's.

In the heart of the growing dream city, within walking distance of the movie lots, was Nelson Evans's studio on Hollywood Boulevard. Photographers too had yet to be tied to the roles they would later play, bound by contract to a studio which imposed its own style and subjects. In the 1920s, each studio would have a portrait gallery as part of the publicity department, with photographers under exclusive contract to photograph its stars in a style identifiable with that studio and no other. Those in the know could tell simply by looking at portraits which company a star worked for – there was the Paramount look, the Universal look, and so on. But these are Nelson Evans portraits, and the people are people who worked for film companies all over town. Yes, there is a look, but it is that which fascinates when one searches the faces of pioneers, inventors, children at play: a look of being the first of the first, a freshness, an intensity that reaches almost poetic heights. Here is Hollywood in all its innocence before the scandals and the smog began to cloud its image.

Stargazing

THREE PICKFORDS – Mary, her mother Charlotte, and her niece Gwynne (*opposite, below*). Evans was not the only man to photograph this most photographed of silent stars, but when Mary wrote her memoirs (*Sunshine and Shadow*) forty years later, the picture she chose of herself and her mother came from

this same session in the Evans Studio. Mae Marsh (*opposite, above*) was a D.W. Griffith discovery whose film career continued up to the 1960s. In this Evans photograph, *c.* 1917, taken in her home, one can almost feel the warmth of California's sunshine filtering through the window onto the actress's feet. Bessie Love

(*above*) got into the movies as a teenager in 1915 and was still at it sixty years later. Painting in motifs on negatives to create dramatic effects was a common practice then. Evans evidently decided that Bessie's youthful appeal and subdued intensity merited nothing less than a halo and a vision of the cross.

EVANS PHOTOGRAPHED not only stars, but producers, directors, writers, designers, and such neophyte hopefuls as were prepared to pay the tariff. This cross-section of his work shows (*above*) Alice Lake, a Sennett star who often appeared as "Fatty" Arbuckle's leading lady, and (*clockwise from top*) two

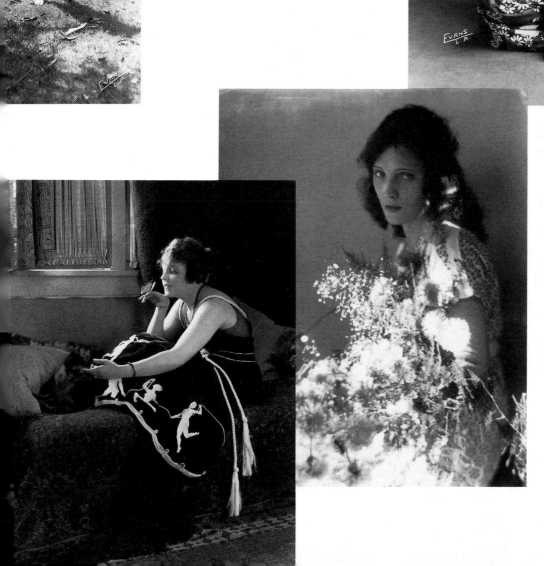

anonymous garden nymphs wearing some inexplicably tattered garments; Tsuro Aoki, the wife of actor Sessue Hayakawa and a star in her own right; silent star Pauline Starke; actress Alice Wilson (who married director Tod Browning of *Dracula* fame); two of Mack Sennett's Bathing Beauties; and child actors Newman and Heck.

BROADWAY 1008
HOME 10634

THOS. H. INCE STUDIOS
INCORPORATED

GEORGIA AND GIRARD STREETS

Los Angeles, Cal., February 12th.1918.

To Whom It May Concern:-

The bearer Nelson Evans, whose signature appears below, has proven by faithful services, when called upon by the writer many times in the past five years, to be a dependable citizen in any emergency.

It is a pleasure to recommend a man of Mr. Nelson's ability, and should it at any time be necessary for him to furnish a bond, the writer will be grateful to be able to give same.

Yours very truly,

James Valentine,
Assistant Manager

Nelson Evans

The Times
NEW TIMES BUILDING
LOS ANGELES, CAL.

Feb, 12 1918.

To Whom It May Concern:

Mr Nelson Evans is not only an exceptionally fine photographer , but is a successful executive and a very resourceful and forehanded young man. In the photography he has done for me he has shown the ability to think quickly and to take quick advantage of situations as they rise.

During the summer of 1915, I was at the front as a war correspondent with the German army. I think I found out about what is required of a war photographer and learned under what conditions he has to act. From that experience and from my knowledge of Mr Evans's work, I can say candidly that I think he meets every requirement.

He has had charge of a large photographic establishment and has shown marked executive and administrative ability.

H. C. Carr,
Sunday Editor.

MACK SENNETT COMEDIES
PRODUCED BY
MACK SENNETT FILMS CORPORATION
1712 ALESSANDRO STREET
LOS ANGELES

February 14, 1918.

TO WHOM IT MAY CONCERN:

In heartily recommending Mr. Evans for any Government or Army position in charge of Photographic work I wish further to say -- that in addition to handling his own Photographic Studio on Hollywood Blvd. he has had full charge of the Still Photo Department of this company and has produced many thousands of negatives and photographs for us.

His work has shown ability of the first order and personally I believe he would be a great value in the United States Service in connection with photographic work.

In handling our entire speed camera and Still Department work, Mr. Evans has shown his ability for efficiency and organization.

MACK SENNETT COMEDIES
By Mack Sennett

People Around Town

Harry McCoy, reading the trade paper *Motion Picture News* on his front steps, 1917. A member of the Mack Sennett comedy team and sometime bit player in Chaplin shorts, he later became a screenwriter.

Suddenly it seemed that everybody wanted to get into the movies. The advice they were given was usually stern. *Photoplay* told one young hopeful in June 1915 that "the inexperienced person, and especially the screen-struck, has more chance of making a living as a jitney-bus driver in Milwaukee than in photoplay acting. New faces appear constantly in the pictures, but there is usually a good reason, and they are seldom the people who have written someone asking how to do it." A new face in Hollywood in 1917 who was there for a good reason was actress Colleen Moore. She had been taken on by D.W. Griffith as a favor to her uncle, editor of the Chicago *Examiner*, who had helped *The Birth of a Nation* and *Intolerance* to clear the censors. Unlike many aspiring actresses arriving in Hollywood, she was sure of a job, but she remembers feeling as nervous as any ingenue: "The trip to California took three days and three nights. I kept asking Grandma to let me look at my fifty-dollar-a-week contract 'just one more time,' until finally she said, 'By the time we get to Hollywood, there won't be any print left,' and she put it in her purse and never let me see it again. I would go to the observation car at the rear of the train and sit on the small open platform and dream of Hollywood. I could hear the train wheels singing, 'You will be a star, you will be a star.' Then logic would pull me back to earth as I speculated on the fact that I had no training whatever. All I knew about how silent movies were made was what I'd read in the fan magazines – interviews in which stars and directors gave advice to hopefuls – and though I'd read every magazine I could get my hands on, what did I really know? Next to nothing."

Some, like Colleen Moore, were successful. Fortunes could be made overnight; $5 extras turned into $5,000 a week stars in less than a year. The film industry advanced by extravagant leaps both in creative achievement and popular acclaim. In three years the movies grew from one reelers to two, then four, and soon were feature length, with accompaniment from live theater orchestras. Yet, for a brief period, the daily routines and appearance of the men and women of the movie industry seemed untouched by this whirlwind change. In many ways the stars were not greatly different from their neighbors in other businesses living on the same block: they too sat on their porches, read their newspapers, went on family outings. For much of the time the local inhabitants could accept the movie people as ordinary citizens. "Most Hollywoodians went about their tasks in offices and shops as before," recalled Evelyn F. Scott, who was brought up in Hollywood. "The difference was that the drive or walk to work might be interrupted by a movie chase or news that your neighbor at the weekly sing could be a star. Next week, for that matter, you could be a star." The only clue given by Nelson Evans's sunny pictures that these are not ordinary people is that they are often shown with film-fan magazines and trade publications.

Of course, this informality is unreal. These are not family snapshots but the work of a professional, who set up carefully arranged compositions in which atmosphere, mood, and lighting were planned in detail. Mary Pickford, Bessie Love, and Lillian Gish had millions of admirers waiting for their pictures; hundreds of thousands of fans would longingly pore over these seductive shots of Theda Bara. For many, the photographs in *Photoplay, Motion Picture Classics, Picture Play*, and the other proliferating monthly fan magazines – not to mention the thousands of newspapers – were an extension of their own family albums. They would be given the latest news of their idols, who were not yet treated as inaccessible gods but as people they might meet or see in their own streets. The stars play with their puppies, pick flowers in their gardens, collect their mail, and even hang out their washing. It is charming make-believe, but quite without the artificiality later to be associated with "off-guard" images of stars deliberately caught "unawares" by *paparazzi*. They pose, but do not pretend that they are dropping their guard, for as yet no guard was needed . . . it was still enough for them just to be themselves.

SOUTHERN
CALIFORNIA'S
climate encouraged
people to stay outdoors.
You could gather
blossoms in your own
garden, as Florence and
King Vidor are doing
here (*opposite*), or take
it easy next to a lily
pond if – like Mary
Pickford (*right, below*) –
you happened to have a
lily pond, or even go
through the motions of
drawing water, Theda
Bara-like, from your
well (*right, above*). By
1919, when the Vidors
had their picture taken
by Nelson Evans, she
was a fast-rising star
and he the talk of the
town as the result of his
independently
produced, written, and
directed first feature
film, *The Turn in the
Road*. For a time they
would work together,
but she retired at the
height of her career to
marry the violinist
Jascha Heifetz, while he
became one of the pre-
eminent directors in
Hollywood. The
Pickford photo dates
from 1918. She had
been the world's
sweetheart for five
years, and though by
then she was earning
over one million dollars
a year, she still manages
to look unspoiled by it
all. Theda Bara,
demurely dressed by
modern standards, looks
rather bemused
standing beside the well
in her garden, as if
wondering what her
press agents will dream
up next. She was the
screen's first "vamp,"
and when this picture
was made, *c.* 1918, was
nearing the end of her
brilliant film career.

BEFORE THEY retreated into huge mansions, behind locked gates and shielded from curious eyes by sheltering trees, film folk could still be found on modest front porches, available to the public's gaze as they worked, read, or went off to the studio. Seated comfortably on a rocking chair in vest and shirtsleeves, Eddie Dillon (*opposite*) looks through a folder of stills, deciding whom to cast in his next film. He was a director at D.W. Griffith's studio, responsible for most of the company's comedies. Bessie Love (*right, above*) was a local girl, née Juanita Horton, who found her way into films as a teenager while still enrolled in a Los Angeles high school. That could well be a textbook she is holding. The newspaper on her lap headlines America's imminent entry into World War I. Louise Fazenda (*right, below*) was one of Sennett's leading comediennes. In her early films she usually looked more zany-like than this modern miss going off to work. Her career as a character actress extended well into the 1930s, before she retired to devote herself full time to her husband, producer Hal B. Wallis.

Front Porches 33

Posing

FRANCELIA BILLINGTON (*above*), one of Universal's early leading ladies, is shown at her Japanese-style front gate, presumably looking for fan mail. Edith Storey, a popular actress until her retirement in 1921, poses amid much porch greenery (*opposite, above*). Exotic, serious, high-handed Alla Nazimova, long parted from wintry Russia, picks a blossom on the grounds of her palatial estate near the corner of Sunset and Highland (*opposite, below*). She was reported to have 47 servants and a permanent orchestra in the house. Long before Dietrich and Garbo, Nazimova wore trousers in Hollywood. A great stage star in the tradition of Bernhardt, she turned to films in 1916. At first movie-goers were impressed by her exclusive, reclusive ways and her stylized, occasionally bizarre films. But they soon became impatient and movies like her all-gay *Salomé* (1923), which she produced and in which she starred, were a financial disaster. She retired in 1925. Her estate was sold to a speculative builder; his bungalows formed a development known punningly as "The Garden of Allah," later inhabited by many famous names, including Scott Fitzgerald.

At Home for the Fan Mags

MOVIE MAGAZINES have always liked to show the stars at home. Nelson Evans was commissioned by *Photoplay* to do a spread on Hal Cooley (*opposite*), who obligingly held a copy of the latest issue while posing with his cocker spaniel in the doorway of his adobe-style house (shown *right, below*). He might be any movie-mad young man across the breadth of America, but in fact he was a stage actor who went to Hollywood around 1914 and appeared in films bearing such provocative titles as *Her Wild Oat, Fancy Baggage, The Little Wild Cat,* and *What Men Want.* Lew Cody's abode (*right, above*) befitted his status as one of Hollywood's busiest leading men from the time of his debut in 1915 until his death at fifty in 1934.

Evans
L.A.

Lillian Gish

Three charming views taken in 1918 of the very private Miss Gish, then twenty-two, at home on Serrano Avenue in West Los Angeles, not far from the Griffith studio. Her mother had rented the house for the three of them, including younger sister Dorothy. "It had a sleeping porch that we used at night," Lillian recalls. "We were working inside the studios most of the time, and we needed fresh air." The house also had a tennis court but otherwise showed no signs of movie-star affluence.

By this time Lillian had been with Griffith for six years and had already starred in *The Birth of a Nation, Enoch Arden,* and *Intolerance* among many other of his films. She was earning $500 a week and could have been making much more if she had moved to another studio. But her salary was clearly sufficient for her to afford a nice car, which was almost as much of a necessity for getting around Los Angeles then as it is today. The picture has been set up to show her house in the background.

39

Pure Hokum

RUTH STONEHOUSE at her home in Laurel Canyon, 1917. She had been making films since 1911 and was described by *Photoplay* in 1915 as "the most popular comedienne the motion picture has yet produced" – surely something of an overstatement at a time when Mabel Normand was already entrancing audiences from coast to coast. Besides starring at Universal Studios, Miss Stonehouse also wrote film scripts and took a hand at directing. Women script writers and editors have always played an important role in the motion-picture business, and for a time in the 1910s and early 1920s women were also active as directors.

These photos were made for a fan-magazine spread. The idea of Ruth Stonehouse pinning up the washing is pure hokum, fabricated for that more naive age when the public wanted to hear and read and see only nice things about their stars. In addition to the houseboy pictured here, she undoubtedly had a maid to do the washing and ironing.

AMERICA WENT
TO WAR on 6
April, 1917, to save the
world for democracy,
and women throughout
the land were expected
to do their bit. Of
course, Hollywood's
stars quickly got into
the act. Serial heroine
Pearl White, famous for
her role in *The Perils of
Pauline*, grew
vegetables for Herbert
Hoover's "Food Will
Win the War"
campaign (*left*). Actress
Nell Shipman (*opposite,
above*), shown here with
her son, kept the home
fires burning for
whoever in the house
has enlisted – perhaps
her producer-husband,
Ernest. A flag with a
star in the window
meant that a member of
the family had left for
active service overseas.
Pretty, long-haired
Margery (later Marjorie)
Wilson is doing some
man's work on the
studio lot (*opposite,
below*). When not
scrubbing floors for the
benefit of
photographers, she
played leading roles in
such films as *Brown
Eyes* and D.W.
Griffith's *Intolerance*
(the Huguenot episode).
She was later a director.

Doing Their Bit

LOUISE GLAUM (*opposite, above*) is reading the ubiquitous *Photoplay* in her garden. She began by playing saloon temptresses in Westerns, usually opposite William S. Hart. In the wake of Theda Bara's success for Fox, Thomas Ince upgraded Louise and made her the studio vamp. When film historian Kevin Brownlow phoned her in 1970 to talk about her career, she said, "Oh, why bother? The films now are so much better."

BEBE DANIELS and her collie "Boy" in 1919 (*opposite, below*). Just eighteen, she had signed a long-term contract with the Famous Players-Lasky Corporation, where during the next decade she specialized in light comic roles. Today she is probably best remembered as the star whose broken ankle gives newcomer Ruby Keeler the chance to do her stuff in *42nd Street*, the film musical that revived the genre in 1933.

BLANCHE SWEET (*above*) began making movies at the age of fourteen for Biograph. Lillian Gish remembers her in those days as being "the most beautiful girl on the lot, a genuine platinum blonde, with the most beautiful hands and feet I've ever seen on a human being." By the time this photo was made, Blanche had moved to Famous Players-Lasky, starring in such vehicles as *The Unpardonable Sin*, *The Hushed Hour*, and *A Woman of Pleasure*.

THREE STARS, THREE
CARS on the streets where
they lived – Bessie Love looking a
bit bemused behind the wheel of
her roadster (*opposite, above*), Ruth
Stonehouse about to step into an
elegant four-door Hudson
(*opposite, below*), and Nigel Barrie
(*above*) about to go off on a golf
date with his wife. Born in
Calcutta in 1889, Barrie had
already enjoyed a successful stage
career in London and New York
when Hollywood beckoned. He
took time off in World War I to
serve in the R.A.F.

Metropolitan Opera diva Geraldine Farrar and her actor-husband Lou Tellegen arriving in Los Angeles shortly after their marriage in 1916. She appeared in six De Mille silents; her artistic celebrity put the final seal of respectability on movie acting. He had been Sarah Bernhardt's leading man when she was sixty and he still in his twenties. In 1915 he went to Hollywood, where he met Farrar. The couple later divorced; Farrar continued her operatic career while Tellegen stayed in films. He committed hara-kiri in 1935.

A Place in the Sun

The Hollywood Hotel

In 1915 more films were made in Hollywood than anywhere else in the USA; by 1917 this suburb of Los Angeles was the undisputed capital of the movie industry, and producing more films than anywhere else in the world. To newcomers, dazzled by Hollywood's dreamland reputation, the unexciting physical reality of the place was often something of a shock. Even quite an experienced actress, like May McAvoy, could be taken aback: "I wanted to get back on the train and go home; that was what I wanted. We were met by a man from Famous Players . . . and we were taken to a small hotel. My mother and I sat down, looked at each other and started to cry. Is this Hollywood? The glamour spot of the world? This awful hotel!"

The physical appearance of Hollywood in the 1910s has been vividly described by California-born Lenore Coffee, one of the very first well-known screenwriters. "In 1919 Hollywood was still a village. Hollywood Boulevard could have been any main street in America. The heat was a clear desert heat. The sky, a strong, deep blue and the mountains like cardboard cut-outs – you could hardly believe they had any backs to them. Behind those mountains was the San Fernando Valley, as yet unexploited, save for Universal Pictures having built Universal City . . . On the corner of Hollywood Boulevard and Vine Street was a very large and beautiful orange grove, and one street down was the Lasky studio with its front lined by a row of lovely pepper trees."

Many who started their careers in Hollywood's early days have recalled how quietly suburban it then was. As silent star Viola Dana said, "After nine o'clock at night, you could shoot a cannon off on Hollywood Boulevard and never hit anybody." Seventy years later this is hard to credit, but contemporary photographs reveal wide, tree-lined, relatively empty streets. "It was a small town," says actress Evelyn Brent, who made her first films in 1914. "Sometimes I drive down to Hollywood and I just cannot believe what has happened to it. There used to be just a few blocks where they had two or three restaurants and one that was open all night where we used to go to eat after we had worked late, at one or two in the morning . . . They had one traffic-cop, and that was only in rush hours. He stood up on a box on the corner of Vine and Hollywood between five and six in the evening and in the morning rush." At night, she says, "it was like being in a deserted village."

The luxurious palm trees and cypresses, characteristic of later views of Hollywood, were mostly yet to be planted. There was no Grauman's Chinese Theater or Egyptian Theater on Hollywood Boulevard. None of the extravagant homes of the stars were yet built. Almost the only landmark was the Hollywood Hotel. Lenore Coffee remembers it as an inviting place, "surrounded by a large verandah with rows of rocking chairs where one could sit and watch the movie world go by. It was really a glorified theatrical boarding house, with large, ragged gardens at the back, but an excellent tennis court. And no matter at what hour one came in, night or day, there would always be someone sitting either on the verandah or in the lounge with whom one could have a chat. Actually it was the nerve center of the town, as well as its grapevine."

This cozy small-town atmosphere was to fade as every day new people swarmed into Hollywood eager for opportunities in the film business. In 1915 there were 12,000 people engaged in making motion pictures there; by 1917 the number had risen to 20,000. Where at first rooms had been hard to find for the influx of itinerant actors, new hotels and boarding houses quickly sprang up to take advantage of them. The newcomers were nervously watched by the existing residents, who became increasingly concerned as the Hollywood Hotel began to cater almost exclusively for the movies and the neighborhood became a backdrop for films of all descriptions. The contrast between the burgeoning industry and its setting was occasionally bizarre: the town's largest building was a film set, Babylon – used for *Intolerance* – rising on the corner of Hollywood and Sunset Boulevards, overshadowing quiet streets that still might peter out amid fields. But even in those fields there would probably be film men, perhaps working out a comedy routine with a donkey. In Hollywood, the movies were now inescapable.

Movie Land

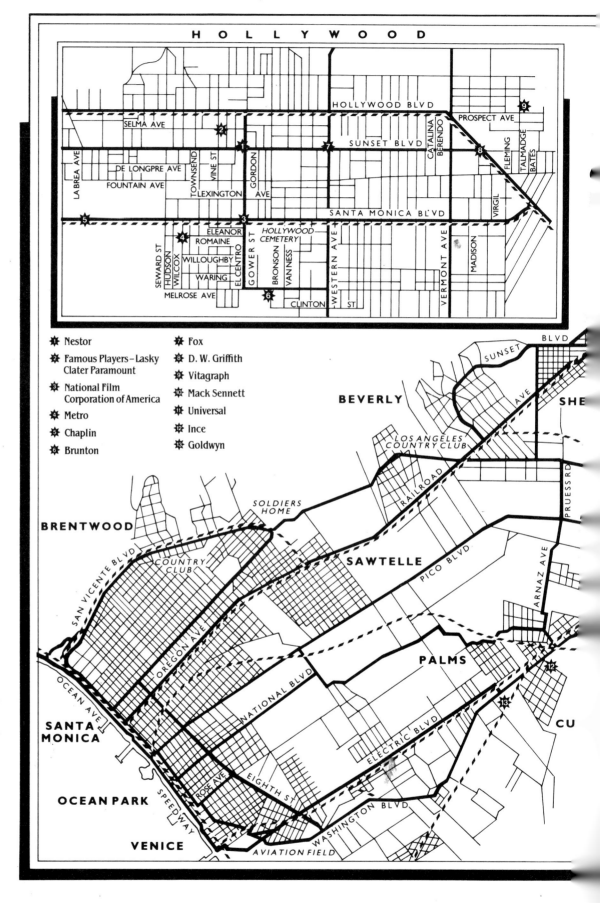

HOLLYWOOD

HOLLYWOOD BLVD
PROSPECT AVE
SELMA AVE
SUNSET BLVD
DE LONGPRE AVE
FOUNTAIN AVE
LEXINGTON
SANTA MONICA BLVD
LA BREA AVE
TOWNSEND
VINE ST
GORDON AVE
CATALINA
BERENDO
FLEMING
VIRGIL
TALMADGE
BATES
SEWARD ST
HUDSON
WILCOX
ELEANOR
ROMAINE
WILLOUGHBY
WARING
EL CENTRO
GOWER ST
HOLLYWOOD CEMETERY
BRONSON
VAN NESS
WESTERN AVE
VERMONT AVE
MADISON
MELROSE AVE
CLINTON
ST

- ✹ 1 Nestor
- ✹ 2 Famous Players–Lasky Clater Paramount
- ✹ 3 National Film Corporation of America
- ✹ 4 Metro
- ✹ 5 Chaplin
- ✹ 6 Brunton
- ✹ 7 Fox
- ✹ 8 D. W. Griffith
- ✹ 9 Vitagraph
- ✹ 10 Mack Sennett
- ✹ 11 Universal
- ✹ 12 Ince
- ✹ 13 Goldwyn

SUNSET BLVD
BEVERLY
SHE
LOS ANGELES COUNTRY CLUB
PRUESS RD
BRENTWOOD
SOLDIERS HOME
RAILROAD
SAWTELLE
PICO BLVD
ARNAZ AVE
SAN VICENTE BLVD
COUNTRY CLUB
OREGON AVE
PALMS
CU
OCEAN AVE
NATIONAL BLVD
ELECTRIC BLVD
SANTA MONICA
ROSE AVE
EIGHTH ST
OCEAN PARK
SPEEDWAY
WASHINGTON BLVD
VENICE
AVIATION FIELD

THIS MAP of greater Los Angeles is based on one prepared in 1919 by the Automobile Club of Southern California for the use of motorists driving to the city's various movie studios and headquarters. Needless to say, Los Angeles has filled out a great deal since then.

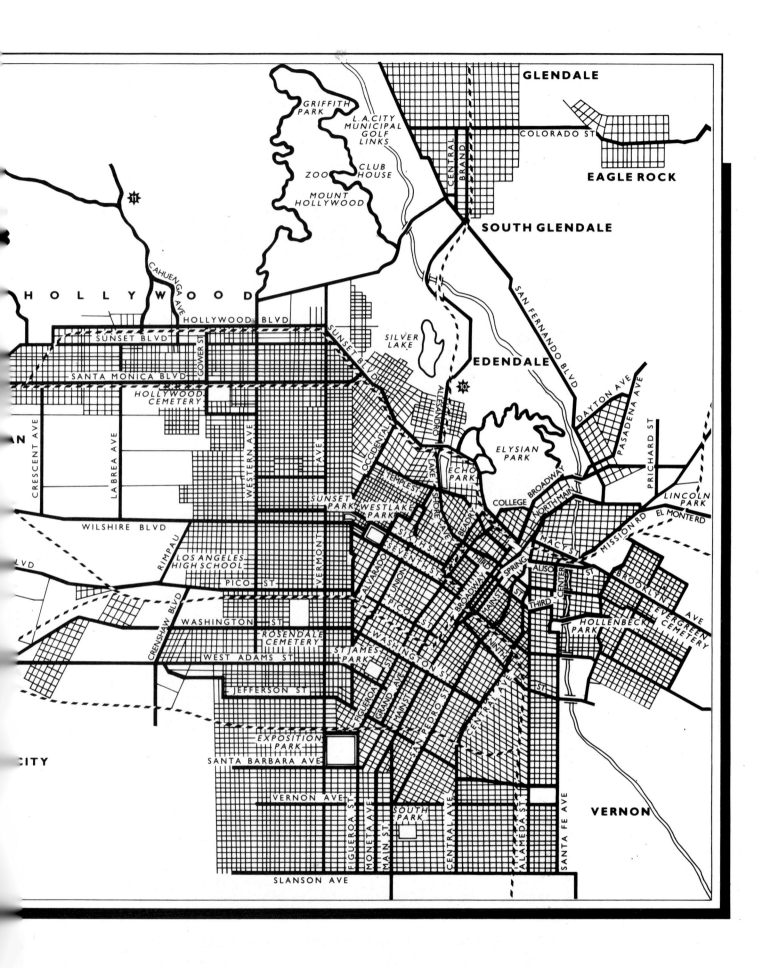

GLENDALE

GRIFFITH PARK

L.A. CITY MUNICIPAL GOLF LINKS

COLORADO ST

EAGLE ROCK

ZOO

CLUB HOUSE

MOUNT HOLLYWOOD

SOUTH GLENDALE

CENTRAL

BRAND

CAHUENGA AVE

SAN FERNANDO BLVD

HOLLYWOOD

HOLLYWOOD BLVD

SUNSET BLVD

SILVER LAKE

EDENDALE

SANTA MONICA BLVD

GOWER ST

SUNSET BLVD

DAYTON AVE

PASADENA AVE

PRICHARD ST

HOLLYWOOD CEMETERY

ALESANDRO

ELYSIAN PARK

CRESCENT AVE

LA BREA AVE

WESTERN AVE

VERMONT AVE

OCCIDENTAL

ECHO PARK

SILVER LAKE SHORE AVE

BRADY

BROADWAY

COLLEGE

NORTH MAIN

MACY ST

MISSION RD

EL MONTE RD

LINCOLN PARK

WILSHIRE BLVD

RIMPAU

LOS ANGELES HIGH SCHOOL

SUNSET PARK

WESTLAKE PARK

TEMPLE ST

SIXTH ST

SEVENTH ST

THIRD

SPRING

ALISO

CENTER

BROOKLYN AVE

EVERGREEN CEMETERY

BLVD

PICO ST

ALVARADO ST

UNION

PICO ST

BROADWAY

MAIN ST

NINTH

THIRD ST

HOLLENBECK PARK

CRENSHAW BLVD

WASHINGTON ST

ROSENDALE CEMETERY

ST JAMES PARK

WASHINGTON ST

WEST ADAMS ST

JEFFERSON ST

FIGUEROA ST

GRAND AVE

MAIN ST

CENTRAL AVE

EXPOSITION PARK

SANTA BARBARA AVE

CITY

VERNON AVE

FIGUEROA ST

MONETA AVE

MAIN ST

SOUTH PARK

CENTRAL AVE

ALAMEDA ST

SANTA FE AVE

VERNON

SLANSON AVE

53

Alterations

HOLLYWOOD as it looked before the movie people arrived can be seen in two photos taken at the corner of Hollywood Boulevard and Wilcox Avenue in the early 1900s (*top left* and *top right*). The area then was entirely residential. The camera is looking northwest in the photo at left, northeast in the photo at right. Between them (*center*) is a view of the same corner, looking west down Hollywood Boulevard, in 1922. A row of small shops fill the site once occupied by the elegant E.C. Hurd house (behind trolley car in earlier photograph).

Middle left: looking south down Vine Street at the corner of Selma Avenue, 1920. The Famous Players-Lasky studio was behind the trees at left of photo. A parking lot and bank have now taken its place.

Bottom left: looking east down Hollywood Boulevard at Hudson, 1925.

Bottom right: looking north on Western Avenue, 1923. The Fox studio remained here as a television center until 1971, when it made way for a supermarket and department store.

Middle right: looking east on Franklin Street at the corner of Bronson, 1918. Franklin is the northernmost thoroughfare in the Hollywood area.

Before the Palaces

THE ERA OF GORGEOUS picture palaces was still to come. In the 1910s, movie theaters all over America looked very much like this – for the good reason that their facades and lobbies generally came from the same source. Architectural supply companies provided theater owners throughout the country with ready-made hardware and ornamentation, and their pre-fab designs were widely adopted. They were among the first buildings designed specifically for movies. The Woodley Theater pictured here is where the locals went to see the latest pictures until Sid Grauman opened Hollywood's first important theater, the Egyptian, in 1921.

The stars featured in this particular billing – Bessie Love, Juanita Hansen, the dog Teddy – are all to be encountered elsewhere in these pages. It is interesting that the biggest billing goes to a short starring Juanita Hansen rather than to the Bessie Love feature.

Street Work

SOMEWHERE ON THE streets of greater Los Angeles there was usually a movie being shot on location, and passersby could watch from the sidelines, or even on occasion take part in the action. *Above*: the great Mack Sennett (in front of reflectors) directs a Ben Turpin comedy. *Right*: Antonio Moreno (arms outstretched) gives dramatic vent to a scene in the latest episode of his action-packed serial, *Perils of Thunder Mountain* (1919). He would later play opposite Garbo and Swanson. The trees were imported to adorn the city's residential sections only a few years before the movies started using them as backgrounds.

More Street Work

HERE WE HAVE Mack Sennett again, showing a trio of bit players how they are to react, while cross-eyed Ben Turpin focuses on the axe in the policeman's hand. Turpin was one of the most popular and highest-paid comedians of the time. *Inset left*: Comedians Earle Montgomery and Joe Rock rehearse a scene for one of their numerous Vitagraph shorts. The lady entering her house at the far right is studiously ignoring the antics outside her front door. Local people took a dim view of such intrusions. *Above*: Unaware neighbors might have been startled to come out of their house and see comedian Bobbie Dunn on the roof next door in what looked like a domestic quarrel but was simply a gag shot for publicity. That's his wife with the rolling pin.

High and Dizzy

MOVIES WERE SHOT ABOVE the streets as well as on them. A favored location for stunt sequences was the southern portal of the Hill Street tunnel in downtown Los Angeles, above which the studio would erect a set appropriate to the scene being filmed. In the flagpole sequence from a Montgomery and Rock comedy entitled *Jumbles and Jokers* (*opposite*) the "roof" was specially built for the occasion, as is evident from the photo showing the scene being set up (*right*). The past master of vertiginous comedy was, of course, innocent, bespectacled Harold Lloyd, shown (*above*) in a scene from *High and Dizzy* (1920) – also shot above the Hill Street tunnel. His companion on the swinging girder is Bebe Daniels.

63

A Montgomery and
Rock jumping stunt,
performed – as was
often the case in the
early movies – without
safety nets.

Up at the Studios

Francelia Billington
entering her private
dressing room at
Universal Studio,
c. 1917. She was the
star of Von Stroheim's
first film as a director,
Blind Husbands (1919).

Once the hopefuls had arrived in Hollywood, their problems were just beginning. In 1915 King Vidor and his wife, Florence, drove into town from Texas. Florence was soon working as an actress, but Vidor survived only by learning to accept what was offered: "I made the rounds of the studios looking for work. I wasn't particular what department of movie-making I landed in as long as I got work inside a studio. I would sit for hours at the casting offices waiting for a chance at an acting job, then move on to the production office and make application as an assistant director, or property man, and, being refused, go to the camera department to apply as a cameraman or assistant cameraman." The Vidors both succeeded, and eventually even opened their own studio. But for most, the story was different, and not as happy. Miriam Cooper, who had starring roles in *The Birth of a Nation* and *Intolerance*, recalled the bench outside the studio "where the extras sat from morning to night, day after day, waiting for a job."

The studios themselves often seemed, in Colleen Moore's words, "a letdown." She worked in "a large three-storey barnlike structure made of clapboard and painted dark green, and attached to it in a makeshift manner were many small buildings. It looked to me as if when they needed more room they just got together some old boards and added on another shack. I don't know what I expected – a marble palace, maybe – but it seemed incredible to me that all the great Griffith films had been made in that ramshackle place."

The studios were especially makeshift in the days before artificial light was widely used and filmmakers depended on the California sunshine. King Vidor has left a graphic account of the arrangement of studios in these early days: "In the business section of Santa Monica were the Western Studios of the Vitagraph Company of America. They consisted of a one-storey corrugated iron building; things were going well: they soon added another floor and, in the lot behind, a couple of open stages. An open stage was a simple affair – a slightly raised wooden platform large enough to hold two or three small interior settings, usually placed side by side. A row of telegraph poles running parallel on two sides of the stage held tautly stretched wires; series of light cloth strips were attached to the wire by rings and arranged so they could be pulled back and forth over the sets to shut out direct sunlight . . . When it rained, work was called off for the day, or the week, depending on the whims of California weather . . ."

The introduction of artificial lights brought some problems. Ince star Enid Markey remembers the effects of working under the harsh Klieg lights: "The next day you would have no 'eyes' at all. That was the only time we had off, when we had Klieg eyes. The remedy was a grated Irish potato and a bandage of cheesecloth bound across your eyes. And you would stay in bed with this and it would draw the fire out of your head. It was a dreadful thing."

The early simplicity soon vanished: Universal Pictures, established in 1915, in two years spread out over 600 acres on the site of a famous battle between Mexican and Spanish forces in the early years of Southern California's history. It employed some 2,000 people, excluding players, and its 88 departments included its own post office, police and fire departments, and the largest privately owned zoo in the world.

Daily routine at the studios was tough. "We worked long hours every day, sometimes late into the night," wrote Lillian Gish. "We filmed all day if the weather permitted, rehearsed after the light failed, then watched rushes." Irene Rich, a leading lady in the 1920s, remembered how in her first years in the movies, she "did nothing but go to the studios, work all day, go home, go to bed, and get up at the peep of dawn. There weren't the restrictions on hours then. You might work till nine or ten at night and they would say, 'O.K. be back on the set, made-up, at eight in the morning'; and you would go home and fall into bed."

But although the life was hard, it is recalled fondly by Hollywood's pioneers. Leonore Coffee was nostalgic about "the marvelous custom of shooting at night during the very hot weather. We would begin at eight o'clock in the evening and continue until four o'clock in the morning without a stop. Coffee was kept hot on an electric plate and there were trays of sandwiches. There was a kind of magic about those nights. They were done only with principals and all went on so quietly. There was a relaxed atmosphere and a sense of intimacy with the medium in which we were working. I think I felt closer to the moving picture industry during those nights than at any other time. And it was such fun to come back to Hollywood Boulevard and eat ham and eggs and greasy fried potatoes at John's all-night restaurant, and roll into bed at five o'clock in the morning."

City
of Studios

FILM STUDIOS were scattered throughout greater Los Angeles, though the area between Hollywood and Santa Monica Boulevards claimed the largest share of them (*see map, pages 52–3*). The old Brunton lot (*top left*), which later became part of Paramount, was typically unglamorous. In the foreground are cameraman Edward Cronjager and stills photographer Frank Powolny, who many years later shot some famous pin-ups of Betty Grable and Marilyn Monroe. Reaguer Productions (*continuing counterclockwise*) and Robbins Photo Plays (*top right*) were small independents that never hit the big time. Metro (*bottom left*) most certainly did, though at the time of this photo, 1918, the merger with Goldwyn and Mayer was still six years off. Kalem (*bottom right*) was one of the first studios established in California. Nearby was Vitagraph (*center*). The well-dressed group standing around in the sun are extras on the Famous Players-Lasky lot.

The City of Streets
Universal Studio

RECOGNIZED BY ALL as the father of films as we know them today, D.W. Griffith was born near Louisville, Kentucky, in 1875. After some unsuccessful attempts to establish himself as an actor and a writer, he stumbled into the infant movie industry, then (1907) still headquartered in New York. Griffith's instinctive creative flair for the new medium soon put him at the top of the profession. In 1910 he began making movies in California, and it was there that he produced and directed the Civil War epic *Birth of a Nation* (1915), a landmark in the development of cinema as an art. *Above*: Local inhabitants couldn't believe their eyes when, in October 1915, this huge construction began to loom over the back lot of the Griffith-Fine Arts Studio. The modest houses (which still exist) at the intersection of Talmadge Street and Prospect Avenue give scale to the mammoth set for the Babylonian sequence of a film originally called *The Mother and the Law*, later retitled *Intolerance*. The site opposite (i.e., where the photographer is standing) was later taken over by Vitagraph

(and, much later still, by ABC Television).

Below: Eddie Dillon (see page 32) in his car, outside the Griffith studio. The bungalow court in the background contained the studio offices.

Opposite: It is March 1918 and Griffith, just back from filming in Europe, is seated at the counter of the White Kitchen Restaurant near his studio. At the far right is

his New York manager, A.L. Gray. The man with a mustache looking at Griffith's newspaper is Bobby Harron, the studio's popular "juvenile" lead. His tragic demise when he accidentally discharged prop bullets into his stomach was one of the first in a series of disturbing deaths of public idols that aroused widespread curiosity and later mushroomed into the scandals that ended Hollywood's years of innocence.

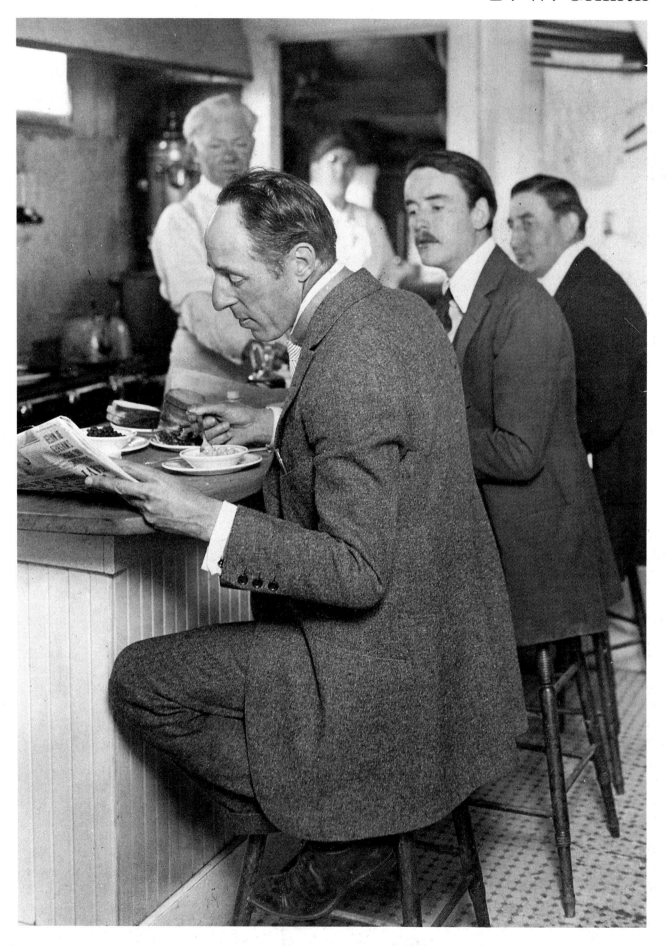

Intolerance

WITH PROFITS BILLOWING in from *Birth of a Nation*, Griffith embarked on the most ambitious production Hollywood had ever seen. *Intolerance* (1916) was said to have cost the then-unprecedented sum of $2.5 million, and for years this figure was taken as gospel. Recent research by Richard Schickel has established its cost more realistically at some $285,000. This should be compared with *The Squaw Man* (1914), one of the first feature-length films, which cost $15,450.75. Even so, De Mille's *Joan the Woman* (1917) cost $302,976.26 – but, unlike *Intolerance*, it made money. *Intolerance's* relative failure at the box office hampered Griffith's career but its influence on other directors was enormous.

Many stills from the mammoth production have been published, but this one has not been seen since it was first used for an article in 1916. The hundreds of extras assembled in this fantasy of ancient Babylon look like so many ants when their hill has been disturbed. Note the scaffolding at far right that supports the set, with another part of the set behind.

Seena Owen, who played Princess Beloved in the Babylonian episode of *Intolerance*, is seen (*inset*) getting out of her roadster in front of the towering sets.

Off Camera

ALTHOUGH GRIFFITH usually headed the pack, he was often never more than a few weeks ahead of the rest, and none was faster than that other New York expatriate, Cecil B. De Mille. For years before he established himself as the master of cinematic spectacle, C.B. was as inventive and creative a director as anyone in Hollywood. He is seen in shirtsleeves (*left, above*) taking a lunchtime break during the shooting of *Joan the Woman* (1917) with the film's star, opera singer Geraldine Farrar, and his business partner, Samuel Goldfish (soon to become producer Samuel Goldwyn); and conferring on set with the leading man, Wallace Reid (*left, below*). Dark glasses were commonly used to protect an actor's eyes from the powerful open-arc Klieg lights.

ANOTHER CINEMATIC giant, Charlie Chaplin, chats with Mutual Film studio manager John Jasper (*below*) on the set of *The Immigrant* (1917). The heavy pendulum hanging from the tripod at far left was used to rock the camera back and forth in order to simulate the rocking motion of a ship's deck in a heavy swell.

"Smiling Bill" Parsons and his wife Billie Rhodes (*opposite, above*) co-starred in a popular series of early silent comedies. They seem to be fooling around behind the set for the benefit of a stills photographer. Parsons was one of the founders of the National Film Company of America, among whose best-known productions were the first two Tarzan pictures.

Enid Markey and Elmo Lincoln, the original Jane and Tarzan (*opposite, below*), on the set of *Tarzan of the Apes* (1918). The public ate it up and the screen's first superhero was born.

ACTORS AND DIRECTORS often posed for publicity shots in between takes. Mary Miles Minter (*opposite*) rivalled Mary Pickford in popularity as the sweet and innocent romantic lead in such films as *Anne of Green Gables* and *Judy of Rogue's Harbor*. Both were directed by William Desmond Taylor, seen holding a sprig of mistletoe over his leading lady. The charming naiveté of this photo is belied by what we know of the principals. The actress looking dewy-eyed at the unidentified young man (probably actor Allan Forrest) was actually dewy-eyed about the older man. All this came out in the wash when Taylor was found shot dead in his Hollywood home on the night of 2 February, 1922. An inquest revealed that the debonair director had been romantically involved with several leading stars, among them Miss Minter. Neither she nor any of the other suspects was charged with his murder, but the unsolved mystery put an end to her screen career.

Above: Priscilla Dean and director Tod Browning – with orang-utan Joe Martin – on the set of *The Virgin of Stamboul* (1920). "Fatty" Arbuckle (*left*) is having his make-up repaired. The girl just may be Virginia Rappe, whose mysterious death ended Arbuckle's career (see page 186).

On Location

THE COUNTRYSIDE outside Los Angeles was ideal for filming location shots. Here, somewhere in sunny Southern California, we see the crew of *Suzanna* (1923), including a violinist and pianist brought along to provide mood music for the actors. The film starred Mabel Normand (next to horse), another of the Hollywood belles romantically linked to the ill-fated William Desmond Taylor. *Suzanna* was to be her last major film; her career – like that of Mary Miles Minter – collapsed following the scandal surrounding Taylor's death. She is shown (*inset*) as the heroine of *Mickey* (1918), a country tomboy coping with the perils of city life, one of her greatest triumphs.

THE MAN WITH PINCE-NEZ glasses standing below the twin cameras (*opposite*) is Louis B. Mayer. With him are his first star, Anita Stewart, and the feisty but superbly talented director Marshal Neilan. The year is 1919, and they are on location at Big Bear Lake for the filming of *In Old Kentucky*. Mayer had recently turned his hand to producing after having organized a large chain of movie theaters in New England. Five years later he would become general manager of Metro-Goldwyn-Mayer, the greatest film studio in the business until all good things had to end.

Mary Pickford (*above*) sits under an umbrella to keep her make-up from melting while filming *Through the Back Door* (1921) on location. Her co-directors, Alfred E. Green and brother Jack Pickford (with black armband – his wife Olive Thomas had recently died), sit in front of the camera, which is being cranked by Charles Rosher. In the background a small orchestra waits for its cue to play – not for the soundtrack (which hadn't been invented then) but simply to wring the appropriate emotions from Miss Pickford.

Mogul in the Making

An American Film Co.
publicity shot, *c.* 1920.
George L. Cox is second
from left; actors pretend
to be his crew.

The Fun Factory

A group of Sennett's Bathing Beauties, including (at the top) Phyllis Haver and (at the bottom) Vera Reynolds.

The undisputed king of comedy in Hollywood's early years was Mack Sennett, co-founder in 1912 of the Keystone company. With D.W. Griffith and Thomas H. Ince, he was one of the three most influential figures in early Hollywood. His trademarks were riotous slapstick humor and the famous Bathing Beauties, the forerunner of all cinema's good-time girls, gold diggers, and pinups. They were created to provide mild titillation for the audiences and huge publicity for Keystone. "I knew that the public – particularly the American public – worships youth," wrote Sennett. "These girls were sweet and cute and adorably young. They made a terrific hit. I knew just what was going to happen; and it did happen. All the one-house comedy companies in the country started to imitate our bathing girls." And, he might have added, many of the major companies as well.

The Bathing Beauties rarely bathed; they were usually near but not in the water. They were pictured clambering over rocks, reclining on long sandy beaches, or perched on dunes, singly or in groups, young mermaids forever on the edge of the surf. Some, like Marie Prevost and Mabel Normand, could swim and dive with professional ease. Even after Marie had been promoted to leading lady, she continued to double for Sennett girls who lacked her expertise. But needless to say, they were hired not as swimmers but as swimsuit wearers. Here we see them as their audiences enjoyed them: cavorting, laughing, posing brightly. Their plump shapes and long-john bathing suits date them – so young, so chubby, so endearingly unglamorous – but their high spirits remain infectious. As Sennett was the first to agree, they often couldn't act, but then, "they don't have to act. Put them in bathing suits and just have them around to be looked at while the comics are making funny. Audiences like to see a pretty face."

The distinction between actress and Bathing Beauty was not always clear to the public. Actresses and comediennes like Mabel Normand, Gloria Swanson, Juanita Hansen, or Louise Fazenda had to explain to each new generation of reporters that they had not been Bathing Beauties, but Sennett's leading ladies. Still, Sennett had an eye for talent; and if, like Phyllis Haver and Marie Prevost, a girl showed more than pulchritude, he promoted her from one of the hundred or so $12-a-week Bathing Beauties to the ranks of the actresses. Most of the girls, however, were never to be remembered for themselves, but always as one of the group.

Even contemporaries realized that the Beauties were not as daring as their reputation implied. As Phyllis Haver has pointed out, the costumes could rarely be called risqué. "Women didn't even have bosoms in those days," she said, "not on the Keystone lot, anyway. According to the Keystone style all the girls had to bind their bosoms like mummies and wear waistlines halfway down their knees." None the less, the censors were a major problem. Bathing Beauty sequences had to be incidental to the film and easy to excise, so that censorship boards in every town of each state could shear the offending Eves from the movie if they thought them likely to corrupt the young. It was hard to predict what the censors would regard as offensive. In Ohio, they compelled the Fox Film Corporation to change the title of their amorous little melodrama *The Devil's Daughter* (1915), because, said the bulge-browed censors, "the devil had no daughter." Added *Photoplay's* editor, "They would have had a much harder time in proving that Balaam's ass never had any direct descendants."

Sennett Land

MACK SENNETT'S early Keystone Comedies – short, largely improvisational, but furiously fast and funny – quickly put him in the forefront of the major producer-directors of the era, and for nearly twenty years he reigned as the "King of Comedy." "The secret of his success," Chaplin wrote, "was his enthusiasm. He was a great audience and laughed genuinely at what he thought funny. He stood and giggled until his body began to shake." Sennett is seen (*inset*) clutching his hat in a vintage Fiat driven by Charlie Murray, one of the most popular comedians on his roster. The Sennett studios were built on the site of a horse ranch in a suburb of Los Angeles known as Edendale.

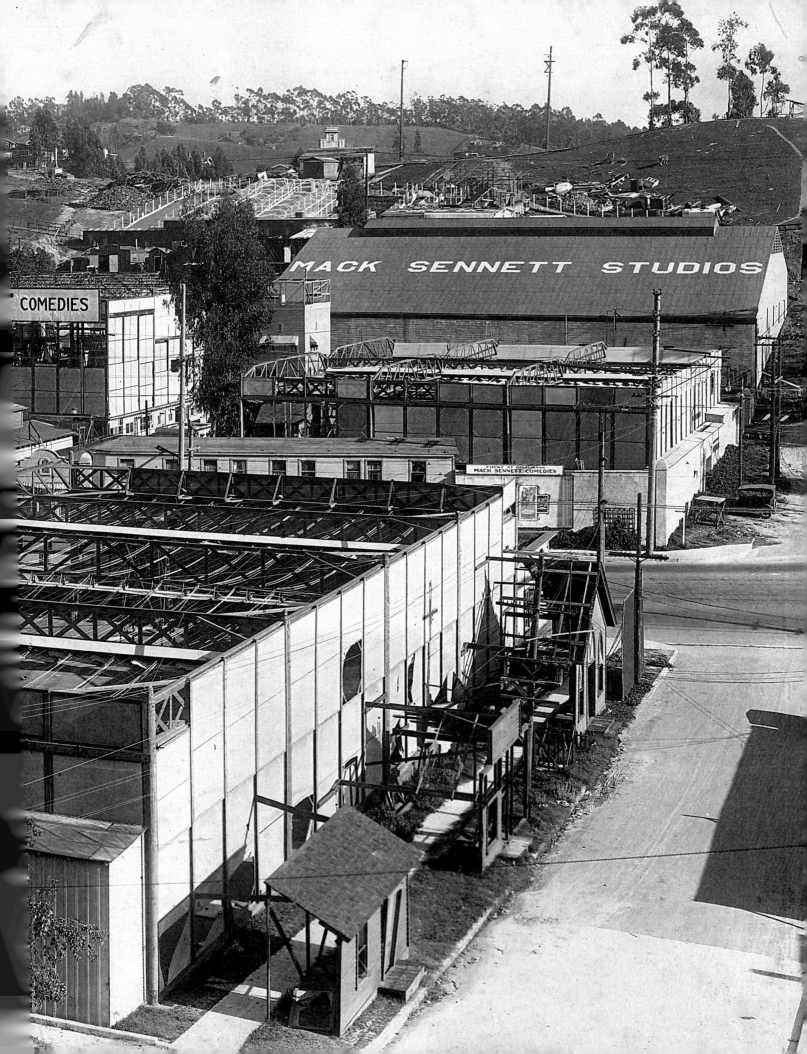

Gags Galore

IT WAS FUNNIER inside Sennett's studios than outside. *Opposite*: Chester Conklin is about to be drenched with a bucket of water, while (*below*) Mack Swain ponders the amorous advances of Dora Rogers. On this page the comic couples are (*clockwise from top left*) Louise Fazenda and Charlie Murray, Mary Thurman ("the premier show girl of the screen") and Al St John, and Fazenda with her duet partner Teddy, the screen's first canine star.

SENNETT WAS AS FAMOUS FOR HIS GIRLS as for his comics. A group of them are seen (*opposite, above*) in hula skirts at Balboa Beach on a day when sunny California was not living up to its reputation for warmth. For the picture with impish, lovable "Fatty" Arbuckle (*below*) they sensibly put something warmer

over their rather skimpy Hawaiian outfits.

Gloria Swanson (seated on stairs with Juanita Hansen, *above*) was a Sennett leading lady before she moved on to become a De Mille star and one of the great clothes horses in the history of the cinema. But in this, one of the several comedies she made for

Sennett between April 1916 and November 1917, it's Juanita Hansen who is dressed to the nines and big-eyed Gloria who plays a tomboy in greasy overalls. Juanita's career was to be wrecked by the disclosure of her drug addiction. She later resurfaced as a crusader against the evil of drug abuse.

TWO OF THESE SENNETT GIRLS were also-rans: Edith Valk (*left, above*), looking disconcertingly modern in her "Annie Hall" dress, and the freshly sprinkled Marvel Rae (*left, below*), described as "the girl with the most beautiful figure" by some publicity scribe on the Sennett lot. It didn't take much imagination to describe Mabel Normand (*opposite*), Sennett's star of stars, in costume here for *Molly-O* (1921), her last great success. In the preceding decade her popularity trailed only slightly behind that of Pickford, Chaplin, and Fairbanks. With a screen personality that was peppy without ever being frantic, slapstick without ever becoming grotesque, she was the prototype for, and the first of, the great female screen comediennes. Adela Rogers St Johns wrote of her in 1921: "Comedy queens and bathing beauties may come and go, but there is only one Mabel Normand. I don't care what they're paying her – even the reputed $7,800 a week. She's worth it."

Tantalizing Two-Reelers

SENNETT TWO-REELERS provided some of the most popular entertainment in the country. In the drawing-room scene here we have flirtatious Myrtle Lind being proposed to by kneeling Al St John while another suitor, Ford Sterling, appears in the doorway. Today Al – who was Arbuckle's cousin – is best remembered as Al "Fuzzy" St John, the grizzled sidekick in numerous Westerns. But what is Teddy, Sennett's wonder dog, doing here? Is he trying to extricate Al before he is caught in the noose, or holding him for Ford, or protecting Myrtle from Al? It's anybody's guess. The girls wearing hats (*inset*) are statuesque Mary Thurman and wry-eyed Polly Moran pretending to be running the studio. On the stairs behind them, Louise Fazenda, dressed as a janitor, is about to interrupt an interloper casually strangling a woman in a striped dress. Both Polly and Louise were character comediennes, and their careers moved easily into talkies.

Bathing Beauties

EVANS
L. A.
©

BATHING BEAUTIES were a Sennett innovation, used more in stills than in movies, and photos of them became familiar eye-catchers in movie-theater lobbies, barber-shop windows, and the more racy magazines and newspapers. Nelson Evans was Sennett's stills photographer for a while, and it is just possible that the straw-hatted man peering down into his Graflex camera (*inset*) is Evans himself.

More Bathing Beauties

"OUR WARDROBE DEPARTMENT supplied what it thought appealing in the way of bathing suits. They sent over high rubber shoes, black cotton stockings, dark blue bloomers, and voluminous tunics with tatted neckpieces and ballooning sleeves.

"I howled in dismay and told them to junk all that stuff and design some bathing suits that showed what a girl looked like. The whole studio turned conservative on me in one of the most unexpected upheavals since the San Francisco earthquake. Even the comedians complained I was risqué. But I went ahead and put the girls on film in the most abbreviated suits possible forty years ago. When the studio received hundreds of letters of protest from women's clubs, I knew I had done the right thing."

MACK SENNETT, *King of Comedy* (1954)

Up From the Ranks

WHILE THE FUNCTION of most Sennett girls was to pose, look pretty, and dodge the pies and amorous advances of Sennett's clowns, a number of popular leading ladies rose from their ranks – girls like Claire Anderson (*opposite*), Mary Thurman (*left*), Myrtle Lind (*below*), and Gloria Swanson (*cut-out*). Right up until her death, Miss Swanson denied ever having been just a Sennett Bathing Beauty, and it is true that she did work for him as a featured comedienne. But since she was a beauty, and wore bathing suits in some of Sennett's films, it's no wonder that future generations added two and two to get five.

Envoi

PEGGY PIERCE AND LOUISE FAZENDA down by the sea for the benefit of Sennett's publicity department.

Miss Reeves, a saucy
Sennett belle, in what
the well-dressed woman
wore to the waves in
1915.

Time Off

Pool party at actress
Ruth Roland's Beverly
Hills estate, 1921. Left
to right: Ruth Roland,
Mrs Reginald Denny,
Kathleen Clifford,
Laura La Plante, and
Helen Ferguson.

People in the early movie business had little opportunity for day-time recreation or a glamorous nightlife. The stars did not yet fully realize how much weight their names carried, and, without unions to protect them, the working week was never less than six days and could even include Sunday if a picture was behind schedule. Working conditions were still primitive and the hours were very long.

But even if the time was available, movie people as yet had few places to call their own. Hotels were being built, restaurateurs were arriving, but the citadels of pleasure were not yet established. This was not the Hollywood of Ciro's, the Mocambo, the Trocadero, or the Mayfair Ball. "When you talk about the wild parties," says Enid Markey, "they took place in the 30s – the 20s and the 30s – but not too much in the 1910s." True, Los Angeles had a thriving bohemian crowd before the movies arrived, and actors from New York, used to sophisticated entertainment, weren't going to settle for a quiet game of pinochle at the weekend. They never saw Hollywood, even in its heyday, as anything more than provincial.

This was still small-town America: people worked hard and long, the games were modest and the atmosphere relaxed, comfortable, parochial. "What social life we had revolved around the people in the studio, for we knew no others," wrote Lillian Gish. "Our lives were circumspect and to an outsider probably quite dull . . . We heard talk of fantastic mansions, custom-made cars, fabulous jewels and wild parties. It was all far removed from our world, where a date ended at 10:00 because one was expected on set, fresh and rested, at 8:00 next morning." Friends went out to swim in the ocean under smogless skies on still unpolluted beaches along the Pacific Coast Highway. They went to the theater to catch old friends still touring with vaudeville or with plays. Mostly, though, they went to each others' homes for quiet dinners. As one of the chroniclers of the era reported, "It was a small town with small people doing small things on small weekends."

Not surprisingly perhaps, the fans found this increasingly hard to believe, despite the reassurances of the fan magazines. "So you have heard some awful tales of how film players conduct themselves on the Sabbath," said *Photoplay* in reply to an anxious correspondent. "I can't tell you much about that. My good friends the Gishes go to church on Sunday; so do some other picture people I know."

The fans' curiosity was aroused by the reports of the sky-rocketing salaries their simple screen sweethearts were earning. There is nothing like vast sums of money to put innocence to flight. It was one thing to read that Mary Pickford was earning $500 a week. She was good, and pure, and worth that, but when it came out that she was going to be making $1,000,000 a year – and wanting more! – although it did not kill affection, it caused people to pry. Yet Pickford survived even the potential scandal of two divorces without alienating her public. Everyone could tell that the Mary they knew and loved had not been changed by fame. In her films and her photographs they saw that face, as fresh and innocent as ever. And indeed she kept on living as she always had, surrounded by those friends, like Mildred Harris (later Chaplin's first wife) and the Gish girls, whom she had known since the time they were all child actors touring the theaters. They had sewing circles and ukelele groups, and they behaved like the very young people they still were. The innocence captured by Nelson Evans was soon to fade, but these photographs contain no hint of the scandals that were to transform the public image of Hollywood within a matter of years.

Down by the Beach

SENNETT'S GIRLS WEREN'T THE ONLY ones who swarmed to the beach. It was a favorite recreation spot for the whole film colony. Bessie Love, cowboy star William S. Hart, and his horse Fritz enjoy the annual Ince-

Triangle studio outing on the sands near Santa Monica, 1917 (*opposite, above*). Virginia Pearson, a popular "vamp" of the day, seems to prefer a more sedate form of locomotion (*opposite, below*). Another beachgoer is teenage

Norma Talmadge (*inset*), who was quoted in a 1916 *Photoplay* cover story: "I take my work seriously. That's why I love to come down here to the shore sometimes and be lazy and do nothing but listen to the sea."

All at Sea

THESE MACK SENNETT GIRLS seem to be getting in position for a race in their tubs. The insets show William S. Hart (*above*), for once without a horse, on the same Ince-Triangle studio outing (page 111), and Annette Kellerman (*below*), waving hello across the Pacific – perhaps to her native Australia. Her life inspired a rather romanticized film biography starring Esther Williams (*Million Dollar Mermaid*, 1952). This Evans photo of the champion swimmer and diver dates from 1918, when she was filming *Queen of the Sea*.

Strumming
Stars

WITHOUT RADIO
or television,
home entertainment
had to be self-
generated. For a while
everyone in America
seemed to be playing, or
at least strumming, a
banjo or ukelele.
Naturally, the craze hit
Hollywood. The large
picture shows the
Flugrath sisters, better
known to their fans as
Viola Dana and Shirley
Mason, attempting
some banjo duets by
the fireside. In the
picture on the wall,
Mildred Harris, a
popular screen
soubrette and Charles
Chaplin's first wife,
solos on the ukulele.

It could be a lawn anywhere in America, but this is Hollywood and the friends on view (*above*) are (*left to right*) Mildred Harris, Mary Pickford, Lillian Gish, Mrs Gish (standing), and Dorothy Gish. Both Mary and Lillian used photographs taken at this session in their autobiographies. Down at the beach (*right*) are Charlie Chaplin with vaudeville star Eddie Foy (pointing), "Fatty" Arbuckle (behind Foy), and Chaplin leading lady Edna Purviance. The teenage girl with the mushroom hat sitting under a tree (*opposite*) is Gloria Swanson before she became a grand De Mille star.

Ocean Park Bath House,
Santa Monica

If Mother Could
See Me Now

Jessie Fox, Sennett
Bathing Beauty and
aspiring actress, poses
coyly for Evans's
camera.

With the exception of the near-nude Theda Bara in *Cleopatra* (1917), the all-nude Annette Kellerman showing off her perfect figure in the 1916 epic *Daughter of the Gods*, and the model on pages 122–3 who may be Betty Compson, the girls shown here – and they include some of Sennett's Bathing Beauties – are unknown. Then as now a pretty girl might pad her meager earnings by modelling for "art" studies. The poses are innocent by today's standards, but they caused consternation at the time.

The moral dangers to the unknown, unemployed girls flocking to Hollywood, whose faces we see here, were denounced again and again. It was a futile attempt to stop girls arriving in the hope of finding fame and making their fortunes only to end up giving Hollywood a bad name when they were arrested for soliciting and their pictures were splashed across a nation's newspapers under headlines like "Hollywood Star Arrested in Vice Ring." They seemed prepared to do anything. Mack Sennett recalled being introduced to a schoolmarm from Vermont who wanted to appear in his films: "When I said 'Let's see your knees, honey,' . . . she heisted her dress all the way and spun around buff-naked."

Many came, few were chosen, and thousands got lost in the shuffle. The letter columns of the film magazines began to read like a missing person bureau. J.L., of Cedar Rapids, Ia., was told in July 1917, "Sorry, but your description is too meager and the right name of the lady is no help to us. She has probably assumed a screen name and her black hair may now be a glorious titian. If you have a picture of the young lady we should be glad to look her up." Grim articles in *Photoplay* cited the sorry fates that met many Hollywood hopefuls. One entitled "The Girl Outside" was headlined "Can the Pretty Girl without Influence Break into the Movies? Most of the Experts Say No!" A girl from the South, "a genteel flower," had killed herself after getting nowhere; numerous others had been swindled of what little money they had. "Some misdirected girls try to break in by the so-called 'easiest way.' A great many have been encouraged to try this route by the gossip about success gained through the ultimate sacrifice and the published newspaper stories about moral conditions in the studio. Time was when unscrupulous directors preyed on the ignorant and innocent but in nearly every case which ended up in the juvenile court, it was disclosed that the offender was an assistant director . . . But the stories circulated widely in the early days are still bearing fruit and many a girl who could withstand the ordinary temptations of life has offered herself as a voluntary sacrifice, in the belief that it was the only way to assured success . . . There is no easiest way."

The magazines emphasized that the life of girls working for the film studios was one of impeccable moral rectitude. In 1921 *Photoplay* published the following set of rules for girls in films, drawn up by Al Christie, among the best-known producers of silent comedy films: "1 Must be between five feet and five feet eight in height. 2 Weigh not less than 100 or more than 130 pounds. 3 On days when not called for pictures, must report for dancing training or scene rehearsals at 10 am. 4 Must not alter color of hair or cut same without permission. 5 Must be at the studio every working day at 8:30 am. 6 Must be able to pass tests for riding, swimming, dancing and social etiquette. 7 Must not smoke cigarettes in studio nor in public places. 8 Must not chew gum. 9 Required to participate in annual girls' hike and other athletic activities. 10 Must possess at least one evening dress, sport suit, street suit, afternoon dress; one pair of dancing shoes, walking shoes, street slippers and hats for same. 11 Must not attend cafés or other public places at late hours except on Saturday night, or when not called for work next day." Other studios were equally paternalist. "The absolute rule that we had," wrote Mack Sennett, "was that if some comedian were going to help some girl get ahead in the acting profession by dating her he got fired."

Mack Sennett's fears for the girls on his lot were justified in the 1920s by the revelations about the private lives of such stars as Chaplin and "Fatty" Arbuckle. The more deadly problem of drug pushing went unchecked. A fairly well-known Sennett actor, referred to as "The Count," was one of Hollywood's major drug pushers. He provided cocaine for a number of stars, including Mabel Normand, Juanita Hansen, and Wallace Reid, one of the most popular actors of the age. Revealing of the changing mores was the tone of the fan magazines. In a reply to an aspiring actress, one remarked "So, all your friends say that you are a natural weeper and should be in the movies. They use glycerine out here when they're stuck for tears, so I shouldn't leave home if I were you." The hardboiled accent of Hollywood in the 20s and 30s is already there.

Nude in Hatbox

The model for these charming nude studies (*c.* 1916) is identified on the negative holders as none other than Al Christie's leading comedienne Betty Compson (see page 175). Although the attribution is open to question, this pretty girl does share the abundant auburn hair, broad cheeks, and svelte figure of the popular 1920s star. Anyway, if it is Betty Compson, she wouldn't have been the first actress – or the last – to have begun her career by posing in the nude.

All in a Day's Work

Although some of the girls on these pages and the next are identifiable, their names don't really matter. They were mostly bit players or extras, hoping for a chance to break out of anonymity, but not until the 1950s did a girl rise from these ranks to the stardom they all dreamed of – Marilyn Monroe.

ANNETTE KELLERMAN, the Australian long-distance swimmer, who also appears on page 113, became the screen's first swimming star. She has only her long hair to preserve her modesty in this scene from *A Daughter of the Gods* (1916).

THEDA BARA, Hollywood's original "vamp," posing ever so daringly as the *fatale* heroine of *Cleopatra* (1917). In Hollywood, antiquity has always been popular as an excuse for undressing. This picture, like that opposite, is by Witzel, a Los Angeles photographer whose work often appeared in magazines beside Evans's.

"Don't squeeze me 'til
I'm yours" – one of
Evans's cheekier shots.

Hollywood Sits
for Its Portrait

Viola Dana, a leading
Metro star in the silent
era.

Mary Pickford was having lunch in a restaurant with her mother one day when, she recalled, a young man approached them. "'Mrs Pickford,'" he said, "'my name is Rudolph Valentino. I want you to forgive me for taking the liberty of speaking to you without having been introduced. I am very eager to have your advice as to how I may get into motion pictures.' The advice Mother gave him – the first of its sort I believe – was later to become standard practice. 'Mr Valentino,' she said, 'the first thing you must do is to get the very finest photographs of yourself. Spend plenty of money on them. See that there are photographs in profile, full face, bust and full figure. On the back of each give your age, your height, your complexion and your experience. Send copies of them to each and every one of the studios.''

Mrs Pickford was right. Soon nobody could underestimate the importance of good portraits in the career of an actor. As well as getting people work, they were a link between the public and their idols. By the beginning of the 1920s, when the studios took over responsibility, stars had spent fortunes on photographs like those illustrated here. Mary Pickford, with the world clamoring for her image, spent the most – an astonishing $50,000 a year – but Lillian and Dorothy Gish had photography budgets of $10,000 each per annum, and it does not seem that they were unusual.

As the film studios developed their own galleries, and the expense of fan letters, photographs, and secretaries shifted from the stars to the publicity departments, the private portrait photographers began to fade from the Hollywood scene and out of the pages of the magazines. Until that happened, Nelson Evans was one of the best. His portraits are his finest work and it is perhaps his pictures of men that are his most outstanding achievement. They are much bolder than the standard portraits of the time. His Lon Chaney, his Max Linder – the great French comic revealing himself as a tragic apache – and his Tom Mix are unforgettable images. Look at Buster Keaton and Rudolph Valentino, in portraits taken on the fringes of fame: they face each other, strong and unflinching, daring you to say which will become the great lover and which the great comedian. The portraits of women, though very lovely, are a little more conventional, posed in a style or with objects that firmly bind them to the age; there was no "timeless" look until the advent of Garbo. In these early days unconventional beauties like Pauline Starke were not well handled by most photographers, who too easily made her large, broad-boned, flat-featured face look old and ungainly. Evans gives her a severe, dramatic look – no frills, just the face – a look that anticipates changing tastes (page 149).

Whether posing as virginal innocents forever on the edge of puberty, or as world-weary bella donnas smothered in monkey fur and too much mascara, almost all the women shown here have one quality in common: youth.

Theda Bara, "the wickedest woman in the world," was in truth no older than "the first child of dawn," Mary Pickford. When Chicago columnist Louella Parsons met Bessie Love in 1918, she didn't hide her astonishment at finding the popular star little older than the children she mothered in her films. In the 1960s, when I met many of the silent stars for the first time, I too was surprised to discover they were thriving matrons rather than the withered crones I had expected. "Darling, I'm not Grandma Moses," said Enid Markey. "I may have been playing mothers in movies but I was only a kid when I played them. Of course, we were very young . . . and that's why people say, 'Oh, I remember her when I was a child.' But I was a child then too!" Those motherless heroines in Griffith's films were, in truth, fatherless children just into their teens. They had to be young. The gauzes and lenses and lights that later gave women in their forties the smooth look of a twenty-year-old had yet to come into their own. It took little to look older but a lot to look young. "The camera was heartless; it exaggerated," said Lillian Gish. "Fortunately, I photographed 'young.' But sometimes the harsh cameras made a fourteen-year-old seem an old hag." That's why the arrival of Broadway star Fanny Ward in 1915 aroused so much curiosity among women, both on and off the screen, for Fanny was in her mid-forties, although she played curly-haired, dewy-eyed young girls.

As well as youth, these photographs also reveal individual personalities. They are very different from the slick, manufactured look of many stars of the 20s and 30s. "People wonder why stars who were well known years ago are still remembered and spoken of with love," mused Carmel Myers, an early discovery of D.W. Griffith. "I think it was because we did not have make-up men. Now I love make-up men; I've nothing against them. But whatever you had, you did your own, good or bad. Your own lips, eyes, nothing changed in your face. Unfortunately, today, there is a sort of assembly-line look. We didn't have that then: whatever was ours, we kept it and carried it." Her views are supported by Gloria Swanson: "Nobody looked alike. We were all originals."

Evans played with light, dramatized with shadows, and idealized his subjects with conventional props, but he knew that true beauty required only three things: a camera, a subject, and trust. People usually gave him their best, as time was to prove. When the silent stars came to write their autobiographies, and cast about for portraits of themselves that would convince new generations of their former appeal, they invariably included those by Evans.

PORTRAITS OF HOLLYWOOD stars were turned out for a variety of purposes – to send to fans, to illustrate features in movie magazines, to adorn the entrances of motion picture theaters, or simply to gratify the sitter's vanity.

Theda Bara (*right, above*) is attending to her fan mail, with plenty of prints on the table ready to go out with her replies. In its May 1918 issue, *Photoplay* Magazine quoted her as follows: "People write me letters and ask if I am as wicked as I seem on screen. I look at my little canary, and I say, 'Dicky, am I so wicked?' And Dicky replies, 'Tweet, tweet.' That may mean 'yes, yes' or 'no, no,' may it not?" (As a result Miss Bara never gave *Photoplay* another interview.)

Irene Rich poses for the camera with a feature about her in *Motion Picture Classics*, a copy of which is obligingly turned toward the lens (*right, below*). The man is Harry Carey, her co-star in John Ford's *Desperate Trails*; he appeared in twenty-six John Ford productions, most of them Westerns.

Mary Miles Minter (*opposite*) is shown – according to the photo's original caption – beside "the daily load of photographs ready for the post office – tangible proof of the growing popularity of this charming little star."

H.B. WARNER (*above*), the son of a well-known British actor, moved to Hollywood in 1914 after making his mark on the London and New York stage. This photo dates from 1920, when he was still playing romantic leads. His most famous role was Christ in *King of Kings* (1927). Later he became a distinguished supporting actor (for example, as Chang in *Lost Horizon*) and appeared as himself in *Sunset Boulevard* (1950).

HOPE HAMPTON (*opposite*), a Southern belle, leapt to brief stardom in 1920 thanks to the backing of Jules Brulatour, a major stockholder in the Eastman Kodak Company, who would finance films on the condition that his mistress be cast as the leading lady. Could Evans's lighting be calculated to evoke a 17th-century tenebrist painting?

Nelson Evans
L. A.

RUTH ROLAND
served an
apprenticeship on stage
as a child actress and
made her film debut in
1911, aged nineteen.
Beginning with
Westerns by the Kalem
company, she quickly
became a popular
heroine, noted for her
athletic prowess in
serials like *The
Adventures of Ruth* and
Ruth of the Rockies. All
of which makes this
out-of-character studio
portrait of Miss Roland
as a bewigged *grande
dame* (*left*) a little
surprising.

Ruth Roland was a
shrewd business woman.
She appears *above*
demonstrating the
merits of Ipana
toothpaste in the late
1910s.

LOUISE HUFF (*above*) was a Georgia belle whose stage career led her to Hollywood in 1916. In her time she often played opposite Mary Pickford's younger brother, Jack, in such films as *Seventeen*, *Great Expectations*, and William Desmond Taylor's *Tom Sawyer*.

HOPE HAMPTON (*opposite*) has more variety in stills than she possessed on screen. The slightly chubby charm she conveys here is in strong contrast to the etherial, rather mysterious appearance Evans had given her earlier (page 137).

CHESTER CONKLIN (*above*) was already an experienced vaudevillian and circus clown when Mack Sennett put him on the screen as a Keystone Cop in 1913. Later, usually sporting the walrus mustache which became his trademark, he appeared in comedies with Chaplin and W.C. Fields, and played supporting roles in such major productions as *Anna Christie*, *Greed*, and *The Great Dictator*.

MONTY BANKS (*right*), né Mario Bianchi, came to America as a teenager in 1914, appeared for a time on Broadway as a comic dancer, then migrated to Hollywood, where he played "little guy" parts in Sennett comedies. Turning his hand to directing, he moved to England in 1928 and married the immensely popular music-hall star Gracie Fields, whom he directed in several films.

143

THREE SENNETT BATHING BEAUTIES doing their parasol routine for Nelson Evans's camera. Just for the record, they are (*clockwise from top left*) Phyllis Parker, Elsie Hart, and Maxine Faye.

ANN FORREST, the girl hitched to a star (*opposite*), was a half-Danish actress (neé Anna Kromann) who worked for several studios, including Universal, Triangle, and Lasky. She acted with Harry Houdini in *The Grim Game* (1919).

R UDOLPH
VALENTINO
(*right*) and Buster
Keaton (*left*), both
photographed by Evans
in 1918. In these
portraits it is not yet
clear that one was to
become a great comic
actor and the other the
great lover of the 1920s.
Keaton had recently
entered films as a
comedy stooge in
Arbuckle shorts, though
he was soon to branch
out on his own.
Valentino, born – like
Keaton – in 1895, was a
new arrival in town,
playing gigolos and
lounge lizards until
screenwriter June
Mathis persuaded Metro
to give him the lead in
*The Four Horsemen of
the Apocalypse* (1921).

EDITH STOREY (*left*) in pensive profile. She started out with Vitagraph and moved on to play leads for Metro, among other studios. Her peasant costume seems unrelated to any of her films. She retired in 1921, at the age of twenty-nine.

PAULINE STARKE (*above*), best known as a leading lady in Graustarkian romances of the 1920s written by the likes of Elinor Glyn, began her movie career at the age of sixteen as a dancing extra in Griffith's *Intolerance*. Unlike many of the actresses pictured here, her face has a strikingly modern cast.

BESSIE LOVE (*left*) is shown in a camera study of October 1919, by which time (aged twenty-one) she had played in some twenty films.

PATSY RUTH MILLER (*below*) was a sweet sixteen when she made her screen debut as a supporting player in the 1921 version of *Camille*, with Nazimova and Valentino. She played Esmeralda in Lon Chaney's *Hunchback of Notre Dame* (1923), and starred in many other films.

AGNES AYRES (*above*) appeared in numerous two-reelers before leaping to stardom as the replacement for Ann Forrest (*right*, and see page 145) in De Mille's *Forbidden Fruit* and as Valentino's leading lady in *The Sheik* (both 1921). In 1926 she was involved in a breach-of-contract lawsuit with De Mille, who said she had become too fat. She reappeared briefly with Valentino in *The Son of the Sheik* (1926), recalling her role in the original, but the top billing in that film went to Vilma Banky, and by 1929 Agnes Ayres's career was over.

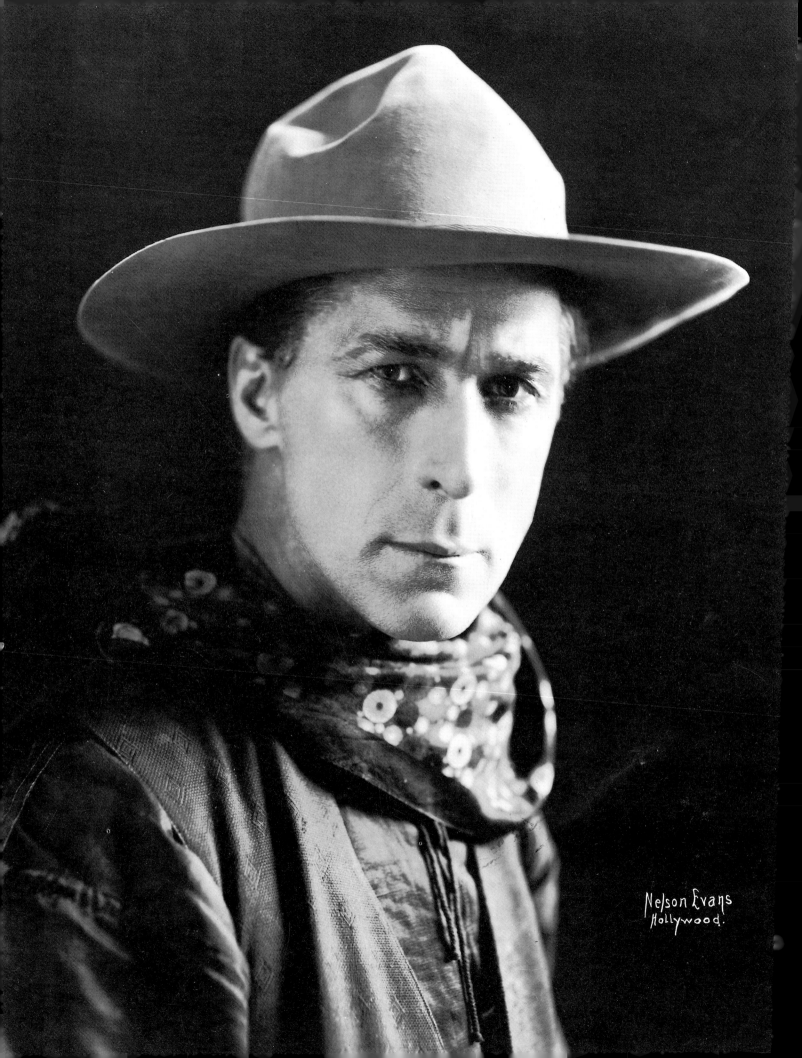

Nelson Evans
Hollywood.

WILLIAM S. HART (*opposite*), born thirteen years before Chaney, in 1870, was already a well-established stage actor when he moved from Broadway to Hollywood in 1914. He was old enough to remember the West as it was in the 1890s, and the Westerns in which he starred (which he often directed) were noted for their scrupulous re-creation of an unromanticized frontier. This photo was taken in 1918, at the height of his popularity. He retired from the screen in 1925, returning only once, in a sound prologue for the reissue in 1939 of his silent masterpiece, *Tumbleweeds*.

LON CHANEY (*above*) was known as the man of a thousand faces because of his superb character make-up and his acting talents, with which he humanized an astonishing gallery of grotesques, most of them in films by Tod Browning (who appears on page 79). He arrived in Hollywood in 1912 and had appeared in over 150 films by the time he died, aged forty-seven, of throat cancer in 1930. In this picture he is in his early thirties, and his great successes in *The Hunchback of Notre Dame* and *The Phantom of the Opera* are still several years away.

WANDA HAWLEY possessed the kind of beauty much prized in the late 1910s and early 1920s. Starting in 1917, she appeared in a number of De Mille productions, such as *Old Wives for New* (1918) and *The Affairs of Anatol* (1921), co-starred with Valentino in *The Young Rajah* (1922), and took the second lead in various unmemorable films. Like many of her colleagues, she retired with the advent of sound in 1927.

ANNA MAY WONG (*above*), born in Los Angeles' Chinatown in 1907, began as an extra at the age of twelve and become an overnight sensation in Douglas Fairbanks's *Thief of Bagdad* (1924). In this Evans portrait she is not more than fourteen, at which point she was already playing featured roles. Her career was to flourish on both sides of the Atlantic in silents (*Piccadilly*, 1929) and talkies (*Shanghai Express*, 1932). Her last film was *Portrait in Black* (1960).

EVANS PHOTOGRAPHED this shot of Betty Compson (*above*) for the pages of *Harper's Bazaar*. Evelyn Brent (*right*) was a Brooklyn girl who broke into films as an extra in minor East Coast productions while still a high-school student. By 1916 she was in Hollywood and beginning to be tapped for female leads. She became a star in British silents, returned to America in the early 20s to play gangster molls, and reached a peak in three silent films directed by Von Sternberg, who made of her a dark-haired precursor of Dietrich.

A QUARTET OF ACTORS (*opposite*) whose careers all bridged the transition from silents to talkies. Louis Calherne (*above left*) began as a romantic, elegant leading man in the 1920s and later graduated to such heavyweight roles as Justice Oliver Wendell Holmes in *The Magnificent Yankee* (1951) and Julius Caesar in John Houseman's film of the play (1953).

Thomas Meighan (*above right*) began on Broadway at the turn of the century, moved to Hollywood in 1913, and hit the big time six years later with his starring role in *The Miracle Man*, which he followed with a series of opulent De Mille society dramas, including *Male and Female* (1919). He continued to play leads in a series of totally undistinguished films into the early 1930s.

Jack Holt (*below left*) was the sort of man the flappers liked best – strong, silent, dependable. This Evans portrait of 1917 shows him near the start of his career. He was still at it, mainly in B pictures, throughout the 1930s and 1940s.

Eugene Pallette (*below right*) will be unrecognizable here to those who remember him only as a jolly, rotund character actor in classics like *The Ghost Goes West*, *My Man Godfrey*, and *The Adventures of Robin Hood*. But during the 1910s, when this photo was taken, he played leading roles in such silents as *Intolerance* and *A Man's Man*.

MAX LINDER (*above*), posing as an apache for Nelson Evans's camera, was a smooth and sophisticated French comedian who arrived in Hollywood in 1916 as part of his first American contract (with Essanay studios), after having been Europe's leading film comic, anticipating the antics of Chaplin and Mack Sennett. Ill health, caused by gas poisoning suffered in World War I, hampered his short American screen career. His most famous American film was *The Three Must-Get-Theres* (1922), a parody of Fairbanks's *The Three Musketeers*.

GRACE DARMOND was a statuesque blonde who appeared in a number of serials and such provocatively titled features as *The Girl in His House*, *See My Lawyer, Daytime Wives*, and *Alimony*. Despite this a fan magazine described her as an actress "mantled with shyness . . . She uses no make-up except a touch of red lipstick which somehow or other fails to lend any air of sophistication." Her career, like that of so many silent stars ended with the advent of sound.

Evans
L.A.

TOM MIX, a real-life cowboy who made good in the movies, began making shorts in 1909 and went on to become the silent era's most popular cowboy star – by 1917 he had appeared in more than one hundred films. His screen career, which lasted until 1935, was the prototype for the cowboy heroes later played by actors like Randolph Scott and John Wayne. Evans's portrait, as with so many of his studies of men, is strong, bold, characterful, both timeless and of its time.

MILDRED HARRIS was nine when discovered for films by Lois Weber, thirteen when she played Dorothy in a series of two-reelers based on *The Wizard of Oz*, and sixteen when she became the first wife of Charlie Chaplin (*inset*). Their divorce was a sensation; she died, forgotten, in 1944.

MILDRED DAVIS played in numerous silent films, often opposite that zany master of visual gags, Harold Lloyd (*inset*), whom she married in 1923. They remained together until her death in 1969.

PAULINE FREDERICK was a well-known stage actress when she started in films in 1915. Quickly becoming a leading star of the silents, she adapted her worldly, mature personality to melodrama and comedy alike.

Joan Crawford cited Pauline Frederick as a major influence on her acting style.

ALLA NAZIMOVA, who also appears on page 35, was born in Yalta in 1879, and studied with Stanislavsky in Moscow before emigrating to the United States in 1905. This portrait serves to underline the strongly stylized, somewhat remote image she liked to convey.

R OSCOE "FATTY"
ARBUCKLE (with cigarette) was not only the baby-faced comic of countless Sennett shorts but also a sober and industrious director of his and other people's films. In 1921 he became implicated in the death of Virginia Rappe (page 186), and the scandal forced him to retire from the screen. Later, under a pseudonym, he carried on modestly as a director of shorts and features. Allan Dwan (*top right*) was one of Hollywood's most prolific directors, beginning with one-reelers in 1911 and continuing to the late 1950s. En route he was responsible for films starring the likes of Mary Pickford, Gloria Swanson, and Shirley Temple. Wallace Reid (with pipe) was an enormously popular leading man who played all-American men in the early silents until his death from drug addiction in 1923.

M ARGUERITE DE LA
MOTTE (*opposite*), originally a dancer before she entered films in 1918, starred in several Douglas Fairbanks productions and married a young Goldwyn actor named John Bowers (*inset*). Although both their careers lasted through the 1920s, she was to become somewhat better known. With the coming of sound neither found much work, but Bowers took it harder than his former wife. In 1936, forgotten, alcoholic, he committed suicide by walking naked into the ocean, and almost immediately passed into legend: the details of his death became part of the definitive Hollywood movie about Hollywood, *A Star Is Born* (1937).

THE LITTLE DARLINGS pictured here formed part of a large contingent of child actors who flourished in the 1910s, normally in serials and features directly geared to juvenile audiences. They are Dolly Heck (*left, top*), Jamie Mills (*left*), and Lucille Ricksen (*above*). *Opposite* are Olive Johnson (*left, top*) and "Baby" Marie Osborne (*left, below*). Virginia Lee Corbin (*right, top*) starred in many lavish "kid pictures" turned out by Fox, such as *Jack and the Beanstalk*. Ben Alexander, with the gun, played supporting roles in the 1930s and later made a career in television, where he became famous as Detective Joe Friday's sidekick in *Dragnet*.

JEAN ACKER (*left*) was a leading lady in the silents, but she is best remembered as Rudolph Valentino's wife. She married him in 1919, before he was famous, but on the wedding night she locked herself in her bedroom and the marriage was never consummated. They were granted a legal separation in 1921 but this did not prevent her using the name Mrs Rudolph Valentino in her films. Mona Lisa (*below*) is as mysterious as her famous namesake. Almost nothing is known about this star of early silents.

FANNIE WARD (*opposite*) was an established stage actress when she made her first film in 1915, De Mille's society drama *The Cheat*. She became famous for convincingly playing juvenile parts although in her mid-forties. Her screen career was brief but her parties remained legendary for years.

173

VALERIE FANNING (*above*) was a typical silent starlet (though the term had not yet been coined) whose picture was taken in the hope that stardom was just around the corner. It wasn't, and her name is nowhere to be found in reference books.

BETTY COMPSON (*opposite*) started out in vaudeville and got into the movies in 1915, aged eighteen, playing the heroines of two-reeler comedies. Her big chance came in 1919, when she appeared with Lon Chaney and Thomas Meighan in *The Miracle Man*, and thereafter she was much in demand throughout the silent era. Although she successfully weathered the transition to sound – often playing the violin as she had in vaudeville – her roles and the productions in which she appeared gradually dwindled in importance, and she finally retired in 1948.

MARY MILES MINTER (*above*) was in her early teens when she began to get starring roles in Hollywood. It's easy to see from this portrait why her innocent good looks made her a potent rival of Mary Pickford.

MARY PICKFORD (*opposite*) and husband Douglas Fairbanks (*right*) were filmdom's most celebrated couple during the 1920s and their lavish Beverly Hills mansion, Pickfair, was *the* place to be invited for poolside parties. Evans's portraits show them around 1919, when Doug and Mary went into partnership with Chaplin and Griffith to form United Artists. Mary used this portrait of herself in her autobiography, *Sunshine and Shadow*.

LILA LEE (*above*), who started acting at five (when she was known as "Cuddles"), was another child vaudeville trouper who became a popular leading lady of the silents. She was spotted on stage by former vaudeville producer Jesse Lasky who hired her (then aged sixteen) for his company. She played opposite top male stars like Valentino, Wallace Reid, and Thomas Meighan. Although her screen appearances continued until 1937, she is remembered today – if at all – as the mother of James Kirkwood, Jr., who wrote a semi-autobiographical novel (*There Must Be a Pony*) as well as the book for *Chorus Line*. Katherine MacDonald (*opposite*) was known as "The American Beauty" during her brief film career in the 1910s.

IRENE RICH (*above*) had her best-remembered part in Lubitsch's elegant *Lady Windermere's Fan* (1927). A real estate agent before breaking into films as an extra in Mary Pickford's *Stella Maris* (1918), she played numerous mature female leads in the 20s and 30s and remained popular long after most of her contemporaries had faded from the screen. She was also highly successful in radio and on Broadway.

MARGARITA FISCHER (*opposite*) was voted Favorite Movie Actress of 1914 by the readers of *Photoplay* magazine but her celebrity did not endure. Of German descent, she dropped the 'c' from her name when America entered World War I. This intriguing picture shows Evans searching for new ideas to enhance the appeal of his subjects. In a period when there was great interest in mediums and seances, Fischer (wearing little more than a swath of chiffon) seems to float out of a mist in the style of a "spirit photograph."

ALICE LAKE began her career working for Mack Sennett in numerous comedy shorts and frequently appeared opposite "Fatty" Arbuckle. Although she achieved a measure of stardom in feature films for Metro and other studios in the 1920s, her career went into a rapid decline with the advent of sound. Evans has captured her in a state of bare-shouldered rapture that anticipates Arnold Genthe's famous photograph of Garbo.

FRANCIS X. BUSHMAN in a beefcake post. Bushman (the "X" stood for Xavier) was probably Hollywood's most popular romantic lead of the 1910s, but his immensely successful career foundered with the revelation of his secret marriage to his leading lady, Beverly Bayne. Bushman's famous physique was put to good use in his best-remembered role, Messala in *Ben-Hur* (1926), for which he refused to use a double in the chariot race. He made his last screen appearance at the age of eighty-three in 1966, the year of his death.

COLLEEN MOORE (*above*) broke into films as a teenager in 1917. In the beginning she wore long curly hair à la Mary Pickford, who had established a vogue for floppy ringlets and misty eyes. When hair and skirts were shortened following World War I, Colleen Moore emerged as the epitome of the bobbed-haired, jazz-age flapper, and became the top box-office star in the country. She survived into talking pictures, and was sufficiently rich to refuse all but starring roles. Later she retired into marriage and wrote one of the liveliest Hollywood autobiographies, *Silent Star* (1968).

GLORIA SWANSON, opposite, was one of Hollywood's most fabulous glamour queens in the 1920s. Evans, who had photographed her when she worked for Sennett (see pages 93 and 103), took her portraits when she first began work for De Mille. She made a spectacular comeback in 1950 as the passé silent star in *Sunset Boulevard* (1950), and in her late seventies took a not insignificant role in *Airport 1975*, in which she played a film actress writing her memoirs – a notion which she made real in one of the best cinema autobiographies.

185

VIRGINIA RAPPE (*left*), eyes flashing, body draped in clinging gold fabric, looks convincingly like someone on the threshold of fame and not just a small-part actress hoping, like so many others, to make good. Instead, on 5 September, 1921, aged twenty-five, she ended up dead at the notorious weekend party in San Francisco that ruined "Fatty" Arbuckle and brought Hollywood's years of innocence to a close.

Epilogue:
The End of Innocence

Gloria Swanson
making whoopee in *The
Great Moment* (1921).

When Sam Goldwyn met George Bernard Shaw in 1921 he eagerly attempted to convert the playwright to cinema. "It seems hardly necessary for us to continue, Mr Goldwyn," interrupted Shaw. "You see, you are interested in art, while I am interested only in money." His irony was unerring. By the 1920s Hollywood meant money. Innocence was over.

"I'm not ashamed to say I want to make lots of money," gushed Mary Miles Minter in 1915, already a star at the age of thirteen. "I want millions of it – millions and millions – then when I have a big country place, I will build a lot of cottages for homeless waifs, and bring them up well and happy. And above all I want the public to keep on liking me, because if they stop I shall just lie down and die." How much did movie stars really get? In 1915, trying to play down growing rumors of spectacular salaries, *Photoplay* wrote, "With the exception of Pickford, Charlie Chaplin and possibly Marguerite Clark, there is no film star in America who receives more than $750 a week salary." Only two years later things were very different and they had to admit it. "Well here we are. The million dollar salary is a reality. Charles Chaplin signed a contract with the new National Exhibitors Circuit, by the terms of which he obtains 1,000,000 dollars for eight two-reel comedies." The riches Mary Miles Minter had dreamed of seemed to be within her grasp when in 1919 she was given a contract with Realart, a subsidiary of Paramount Pictures, which was to pay her $1,300,000 over three years. According to *Photoplay*, "her contract stipulates that the young star is not to become a 'public figure' except in the ways that the studio evangelists direct. She can be interviewed seldom, if ever – except as part of said evangelism. She must be seen very little in public – if at all. AND SHE MUST NOT MARRY!"

Despite this protection, Mary Miles Minter's career collapsed in one of the sensational scandals in the early 20s that permanently altered Hollywood's reputation. The first star to fall was "Fatty" Arbuckle, only two years after it was reported that "he has signed with Paramount for the next three years, and the money involved is said to be $3,000,000. We can't call him 'Fatty' anymore." But on Saturday 10 September, 1921, the *San Francisco Chronicle* made public the death of a Hollywood starlet, twenty-five-year-old Virginia Rappe. She had sustained internal injuries at a party given by Arbuckle, and it was alleged that they were the result of a sexual assault by the star. Although Arbuckle was eventually acquitted of manslaughter, his acting career was over. "Universal, on the heels of the Roscoe Arbuckle case, has come forward with an announcement that it has inserted a 'morality clause' into all its present and future contracts," *Photoplay* informed its scandalized public. "In effect, the clause says that any actor or actress who commits any act tending to offend the community or outrage

Hollywood Boulevard
by night, 1936.

BANK OF AMERICA
GUARANTY BUILDING
HOLLYWOOD'S FINEST OFFICE BLDG.
OFFICES TO LET
SECURITY BANK
SLOAT & DENNIS
VINE ST

public morals and decency will be given five days notice of the cancellation of his contract with the company." But only a few months later, the murder of director William Desmond Taylor (see pages 78–9) rocked Hollywood again. The circumstances of his death are still unknown, but the inquest brought to light his relationships with stars Mary Miles Minter and Mabel Normand, and ended their careers.

When I first met some of the silent era stars, I asked them about the scandals that had so suddenly transformed the public's view of Hollywood. They consistently claimed that they had known nothing about them except for what they had read. They denied that the fast living that characterized Hollywood at the end of the 1920s existed at that time. At first I thought they were being coy and evasive but I soon realized they were telling the truth about what they knew – life on their block, in their studio, among their friends. Everything happened so quickly, the industry grew so rapidly, and they had been so busy with work or their quiet domestic lives that it took them some time to understand how the movie business had changed. Now Hollywood provided images of glamour, excitement, and wealth that could not be matched by war-worn Europe. The Arbuckle scandal made the natives of Hollywood realize how the place was seen by the outside world – a dream center, in which the stars were alluring gods and goddesses whose every move would now be scrutinized and held up to the world.

In the aftermath of the first scandals, Hollywood's people and their activities were elevated to semi-mythic status. Mary Pickford married Douglas Fairbanks; they went on a honeymoon around the world, only to be terrified into locking themselves into their hotel rooms when besieged by hundreds of thousands of fans wherever they went, even as far away as Moscow. Gloria Swanson made a film in France, married an unknown marquis, and came home to a triumphal welcome of a kind previously only accorded to heroes returning from battle. Valentino died, and in the grief that struck the nation, several women killed themselves and New York City's police force was taxed to its utmost in controlling the sorrowing crowds. Stars were a breed of celebrity that had never existed before; their popularity set the standard for man's adulation for his fellow man in this century.

Nelson Evans had ceased to be an important photographer by the time Hollywood became the center of world illusion. For a time he had photographed nearly everybody, but by 1921 he was photographing very few, and after that his pictures hardly appear in magazines at all. Who was he? What happened to him? I have no way of knowing. But when Hollywood was still young, he was one of the first and one of the best to capture it and keep it forever fresh.

Acknowledgments

MY THANKS ARE DUE to all the people along the way who helped to make this book possible. I would particularly like to mention David Chierichetti, who fourteen years ago told me of the collection of more than 1,800 original glass-plate negatives by Nelson Evans, the source of most of the pictures in this book. Even then, I felt that the work of this little-known photographer deserved to be rediscovered, and enjoyed by others. Kevin Brownlow's work on the silent era, and especially his book *The Parade's Gone By* (London, 1968), created an audience for the subject.

For facts and figures, and for additional photographs, I am indebted to the time and memories of Evelyn Brent, Dorothy Gish, Dagmar Godowsky, Bessie Love, May McAvoy, Enid Markey, Colleen Moore, Irene Rich, Eddie Sutherland, Gloria Swanson, and King Vidor. Kevin Brownlow and Marc Wanamaker were generous with their expertise when vetting facts. Bill Gibb's visual sense and flair contributed greatly when it was time to make a choice from hundreds of photographs; he made me see again things I had forgotten.

The following books served as reference and for additional quotations: Lenore Coffee, *Storyline* (London, 1973); Lillian Gish, *The Movies, Mr Griffith and Me* (Englewood Cliffs and London, 1969); Mary Pickford, *Sunshine and Shadow* (New York, 1954; London, 1956); Richard Schickel, *D.W. Griffith and the Birth of Film* (London, 1984); Evelyn F. Scott, *Hollywood When Silents Were Golden* (New York, 1972); Mack Sennett, *King of Comedy* (New York, 1954; London, 1955); King Vidor, *A Tree is a Tree* (New York, 1953; London, 1954); and DeWitt Bodeen, 'All the Sad Young Bathing Beauties', in *Focus on Film*, 19 (Autumn, 1974). Besides these, I drew – with enormous pleasure – on more than one hundred pre-1921 American film magazines, including *Photoplay, Picture Play, Motion Picture Classics,* and *Motion Picture Magazine.*

The provision of additional stills was made possible by the helpfulness of Mary Corliss, Stills Librarian of the Museum of Modern Art; Maxine Flecker, of the State Historical Society of Wisconsin; Bessie Love; Mrs Cecilia Presley, of the De Mille estate; Irene Rich; Bruce Torrence; and Marc Wanamaker, of the Bison Archives.

This book is dedicated to my friends and to the staff of the Kobal Collection, who had to put up with my traumas while I was working on it.

JOHN KOBAL   *31 December, 1984*

Index

Page numbers in *italic* refer to illustrations